S0-AGI-180

The Health Insurance Primer

Study Guide

For Use in the HIAA Course
Fundamentals of
Health Insurance, Part A

The Health Insurance Association of America
Washington, DC 20004-1109

© 2000 by the Health Insurance Association of America
All rights reserved. Published 2000
Printed in the United States of America

ISBN 1-879143-50-X

CONTENTS

HOW TO USE THIS STUDY GUIDE

This study guide has two purposes:

- to indicate to the student what information and concepts are most important, and

- to help the student learn and understand that material.

The study guide should be used by those taking the examination for the HIAA course *Fundamentals of Health Insurance, Part A*. It is also recommended to anyone who wants to thoroughly master the material presented in *The Health Insurance Primer*.

If I know the answers to all of the questions in the study guide, will I pass the HIAA examination?

The study guide covers all the important points asked about in the examination. So, although we cannot make any guarantees, if you truly know and understand all of these points, you should pass the exam without difficulty.

Of course, the questions on the exam will not be the same as those in the study guide. They may be phrased differently, they may ask about a different aspect of the same point, or they may require you to apply your knowledge to solve a problem. This means you must really learn the material, not just go through the study guide once.

What is the best way to use the study guide?

We recommend the following approach:

- Read a chapter of the textbook.

- Read the questions in the study guide and answer them to yourself.

- As you answer the questions, check the correct answers at the end of each chapter.

- Mark any questions you were not able to answer correctly and review them.

- If you do not understand an answer, reread the corresponding section of the textbook.

- If you miss a lot of the questions for a section, reread that section.

- Before you take the test, thoroughly review all questions to make sure you can answer them correctly.

If I do not understand an answer and want to reread the textbook, how can I find the right page?

The title of each section of the study guide includes the page numbers of the corresponding section of the textbook.

Do I need to write down the answers to the questions?

No. As long as you check your answers against the correct answers, you do not need to write them out.

Of course, everyone has different studying styles, and some students may prefer to write out their answers. However, it should be kept in mind that, because the study guide covers all the important points in the textbook, there are many questions. Writing out the answer to every question may be very time consuming. If you like to write, you may want to consider a compromise approach, such as writing out only the information you find particularly difficult to remember or that you want to organize and clarify for yourself.

Why are vocabulary questions marked with an icon? ◆

This is strictly for your convenience. Some students like to study all the vocabulary of a chapter at one time so they can compare and contrast terms. The use of the icon enables you to find all vocabulary items easily while at the same time allowing those items to be presented along with the information and concepts they relate to, instead of separately and out of context at the end of the chapter.

What are the practice exam questions at the end of each chapter?

These are questions in the multiple-choice format of the actual examination. The purpose of including them is to enable students to become accustomed to this format.

FREQUENTLY ASKED QUESTIONS ABOUT THE EXAMINATION

What material is covered in the examination?

The 18 chapters of the textbook, *The Health Insurance Primer*.

What is the format of the questions of the exam?

All questions are four-part multiple choice. See the practice exam questions at the end of each chapter of the study guide for examples.

A few questions are multiple-option multiple choice. An example:

Medical expense policies usually have
I. deductibles.
II. coinsurance.
III. overall maximums.

a. I and II only.

b. I and III only.

c. II and III only.

d. I, II, and III.

(The correct answer is d.)

What are application questions?

Questions that require you to apply your knowledge. An example:

John has an insurance policy with a $500 deductible. He incurs an expense of $1,200, which is covered by the policy. If this is his first covered expense this year, how much will his insurance company reimburse him?

a. $500.

b. $700.

c. $1,200.

d. $1,700.

(The correct answer is b.)

You should be able to apply your knowledge of how a deductible works to answer the question.

How many questions are on the test and how much time do I have?

There are 75 questions. You have two hours.

Are there questions on the statistics and numbers in the textbook?

Yes, but not very many. In the case of some simple and important numbers the exact figure must be known. In other cases, an approximate idea of the number is sufficient. The questions of the study guide serve as an indication of what numbers we consider important and what degree of precision is required. However, we will provide two examples to illustrate our general approach to numbers.

- Under HIPAA, the look-back period for preexisting conditions is six months. The student is expected to know this number.

- About 70 percent of Americans have private health insurance. The student is expected to have only an approximate idea of this number. The question would not ask whether the percentage is 65, 70, 75, or 80 percent, but rather whether it is 25, 50, 70, or 95 percent, or perhaps whether a minority, about half, a majority, or nearly all Americans have such coverage.

Is information from figures and tables covered in the exam?

Yes, information from the figures and tables of the 18 chapters are covered, but the basic facts, not the details, are tested. Take the example of a graph comparing different kinds of insurance in terms of number of policies sold. The exam question might ask which kind is most popular. It would not ask how many policies of a particular kind were sold. As with number questions, the study guide should be used as an indication of what information is considered important.

I have a lot of experience in insurance. Can I pass the exam without reading the textbook or studying?

Possibly, but you should be aware that the examination is based on the most common practices in the insurance industry. What your company does may differ. The safest approach is to read the textbook and see if you can answer the questions in the study guide. This will go very quickly if you already have a lot of knowledge.

1 AN INTRODUCTION TO INSURANCE

Introduction (Page 1)

1. What are the four basic risk management strategies?

2. Which of the four basic risk management strategies is used in each of these situations?

   a. James, after watching an airplane crash on the evening news, decides to deal with the risk of air travel by never flying again.

   b. Carmen, after watching a documentary about lung cancer, decides to stop smoking.

   c. Phil, a student, is worried about a recent rash of bicycle thefts on campus but decides to do nothing about it. If his bicycle is stolen, he will use his own money to buy a new one.

   d. Karen buys her first house and at the same time buys fire insurance.

Insurance: What It Is and How It Works (Page 2)

3. Insurance is a means of eliminating or reducing (the possibility of a hazard occurring / the financial loss that an individual suffers from a hazard).

4. Insurance works essentially by (reducing the risk of a hazard / sharing the loss resulting from a hazard).

5. When an insurance company compensates an insured for a loss, where does the money ultimately come from?

Basic Insurance Terms (Page 2)

6. Match these terms with the sentences defining them: **benefit, claim, coverage, hazard, insurance, insured, insurer,** and **premiums.**

   a. An event that can result in suffering, death, and/or financial loss.

   b. A contractual arrangement that states that the insurer will make a payment to the insured if a certain event occurs.

   c. An organization that sells an insurance coverage.

   d. A person or organization that receives insurance coverage.

   e. A payment made by an insurer to an insured to compensate for a loss covered by their contractual agreement.

f. A demand by an insured for payment of a benefit.

g. Payments made by the insured to the insurer in exchange for coverage.

h. An arrangement of risk management by which an insured shares the costs of possible economic loss with other insureds.

The Principles of Insurance (Pages 3–5)

7. What are the five basic conditions that must be met for insurance to operate successfully?

8. Which of the five basic conditions necessary to insurance is *not* met in the following circumstances?

   a. Steve owns a Mercedes and wants to insure it for the same premium rate as Charles, who owns a Honda.

   b. Susan decides not to buy health insurance because she does not want to pay the premiums. She then discovers she has diabetes and seeks coverage to pay for her medical bills.

   c. Jonathan, needing money, burns his house down and tries to collect from his fire insurance.

   d. Helen seeks insurance to cover the loss of a small barbecue grill that she leaves outside.

   e. Bernard has a collection of personal letters that have no commercial value. He seeks insurance to compensate him for the loss of their sentimental value if he loses them.

   f. Phyllis and George are oceanographers. They seek coverage for death or injury during a certain type of undersea exploration that very few people undertake.

9. Why does it make no sense to buy or sell insurance to protect against an event that is predictable?

10. An insurer provides coverage to William to compensate his family for the financial loss they would suffer if he died. Since it is impossible to determine the exact amount of that financial loss, how would the amount of benefit paid to the family be decided?

11. An insurance company has no way of knowing if any particular person will suffer a serious and costly illness. How then does a company know how much to charge an individual in premiums so that it takes in enough money to pay the costs of any illness?

12. Why is it not efficient for an individual to insure an object that costs $50?

13. Which of the following describe **speculative risk** and which describe **pure risk**?

   a. A person accepts the risk of loss in return for the possibility of gain.

   b. There is no possibility of gain. The only possibilities are loss or no loss.

   c. Loss is due to unforeseen and unexpected hazards that are beyond the control of the one for whom the risk exists.

    d. Loss and gain may depend on the actions of the person taking the risk.

    e. Insurance is designed to manage this kind of risk.

14. Which of the following situations are examples of speculative risk and which are examples of pure risk?

    a. Phillip works in a hazardous job.

    b. Roger invests money in his own business.

    c. Jill goes scuba diving for fun.

    d. Joanne buys stocks on the Internet.

The Major Types of Insurance (Pages 5–7)

15. What are the four major types of insurance policies?

16. In **individual insurance,** who is the policyholder?

17. In **group insurance,** who is the policyholder?

18. In individual insurance, who is covered by the policy?

19. In group insurance, who is covered by the policy?

20. In individual insurance, who pays the premiums?

21. In group insurance, who pays the premiums?

22. What is **personal insurance**?

23. What are the two types of personal insurance?

24. Life insurance pays benefits in the event of the death of the insured. Who are these benefits paid to?

25. The most common type of life insurance is (ordinary life insurance / credit life insurance / annuity contracts).

26. What are the two types of ordinary life insurance?

27. Which of the following describe **permanent life insurance** and which describe **term life insurance**?

    a. Generally offers protection for a specified period of time.

    b. Offers protection for the entire life of the insured.

    c. Is also known as "whole life" insurance.

    d. Builds up cash value and is used as a way to save money.

    e. Does not usually build up cash value.

28. What is the purpose of **credit life insurance**?

29. What is the purpose of **annuity contracts**?

30. What is the purpose of **property insurance**?

31. What is the purpose of **casualty insurance**?

32. Why are property and casualty insurance normally grouped together?

33. What are the two types of property losses covered by property insurance?

34. Josh owns a house divided into two apartments. He lives in one apartment and rents out the other. A flood severely damages the house and makes it uninhabitable for a time. Which of the following losses are direct and which are indirect?

    a. The cost of repairing the house.

    b. Josh's loss of rental income during the time the house was uninhabitable.

    c. The cost of replacing objects looted from the house while it is in disrepair and insecure.

    d. The amount Josh spent to rent an apartment for himself while the house was uninhabitable.

35. Albert and Cynthia are in an automobile accident. Both cars are damaged. It is determined that Albert is legally liable for the damage to Cynthia's car. (Casualty / Property) insurance would reimburse Albert for the cost of repairing Cynthia's car.

36. (Casualty / Property) insurance would reimburse Albert for the cost of repairing his own car.

Needs Met by Health Insurance (Pages 7–8)

37. What do the following coverages pay for?

    a. Medical expense insurance.

    b. Supplemental insurance.

    c. Disability income insurance.

    d. Long-term care insurance.

38. What are the two major reasons that the need for long-term care insurance is increasing?

Practice Exam Questions

1. Insurance is an example of which risk management strategy?

   a. Assumption of risk.

   b. Elimination of risk.

   c. Reduction of risk.

   d. Transferring of risk.

2. Insurance is designed to manage

   a. pure risk only.

   b. speculative risk only.

   c. both pure and speculative risk.

   d. neither pure nor speculative risk.

3. Which type of life insurance policy builds up cash value and may be used as a way to save money?

   a. Annuity contracts.

   b. Credit life insurance.

   c. Term life insurance.

   d. Whole life insurance.

4. For there to be "uncertainty of loss," the loss must be
   I.   unpredictable.
   II. extremely unlikely.
   III. beyond the control of the insured.

   a. I and II only.

   b. I and III only.

   c. II and III only.

   d. I, II, and III.

Answers

1. • Assumption of a risk (taking no action in advance and suffering a loss if it occurs);

   • elimination of a risk by avoiding its cause;

   • reduction of a risk by taking steps that minimize (but do not eliminate) the likelihood that the hazard will occur; and

   • transferring all or a part of the risk to another entity, such as an insurance company, in return for payment of a premium.

2. a. Elimination of risk by avoiding its cause.

   b. Reduction of risk by taking steps that minimize the likelihood that the hazard will occur.

   c. Assumption of risk.

   d. Transferring risk.

3. The financial loss that an individual suffers from a hazard.

4. Sharing the loss resulting from a hazard.

5. The premiums of all the insureds.

6. a. Hazard.

   b. Coverage.

   c. Insurer.

   d. Insured.

   e. Benefit.

   f. Claim.

   g. Premiums.

   h. Insurance.

7. Uncertainty of loss, measurability of loss, a large number of risks, a significant size of potential loss, and an equitable method of sharing the risk.

8. a. An equitable method of sharing risk.

   b. Uncertainty of loss.

   c. Uncertainty of loss.

   d. A significant size of potential loss.

   e. Measurability of loss.

   f. A large number of risks.

9. If a loss is a certainty, the insurer must charge the insured the full amount that it would soon be called upon to pay, plus a charge for its services, so that the insured would actually pay more than if he were not insured.

10. An approximate amount will be agreed upon in advance.

11. The company insures large numbers of people and can, based on past experience, make a reasonable estimate of the total number of people out of a large number who will incur medical expenses.

12. The insurer must charge premiums to pay not only for a loss but also for the administrative expenses of handling the transaction. Since administrative costs are almost as much for a $50 loss as for a much larger loss, this is not a very efficient use of insurance.

13. a. Speculative risk.

    b. Pure risk.

    c. Pure risk.

    d. Speculative risk.

    e. Pure risk.

14. a. Pure risk.

    b. Speculative risk.

    c. Pure risk.

    d. Speculative risk.

15. Life, health, property, and casualty.

16. A private person.

17. A group or business.

18. The policyholder (and in some cases her dependents).

19. The members of the group or employees of the business.

20. The policyholder.

21. The group (or employer), the members (or employees), or both.

22. Insurance that covers a particular person.

23. Life and health insurance.

24. The beneficiary, a person designated by the insured.

25. Ordinary life insurance.

26. Permanent and term.

27. a. Term.

   b. Permanent.

   c. Permanent.

   d. Permanent.

   e. Term.

28. To pay down the balance of loans that may be outstanding if a borrower dies.

29. To guarantee payments to a designated party for a specific time period or for life. They often are used to provide retirement income or income for a surviving spouse.

30. To compensate for loss of and damage to homes, buildings, and other physical items.

31. To protect the insured against costs arising from legal liabilities.

32. They are not personal insurance.

33. Direct and indirect.

34. a. Direct.

   b. Indirect.

   c. Direct.

   d. Indirect.

35. Casualty insurance.

36. Property insurance.

37. a. The cost of medical care, including doctors' bills, hospital charges, and surgery.

   b. Those costs of hospitalization and medical care that are not covered by medical expense insurance as well as the cost of other types of care (such as dental and vision care) that medical expense insurance does not usually cover at all.

   c. Living expenses in the event the insured is not able to earn a full salary because of sickness or injury.

   d. The cost of care in a nursing home or care provided at home by a nurse or home health practitioner.

38. • The likelihood of needing long-term care insurance increases with age, and the U.S. population is aging.

   • Smaller families, divorce, and the geographic dispersal of families have resulted in more older people being in situations where there are no family caregivers and paid professional care is the only alternative.

Answers to Practice Exam Questions

1. d

2. a

3. d

4. b

2 THE INSURANCE INDUSTRY

The Importance of the Life and Health Insurance Industry in the United States (Pages 9–12)

1. The large majority of health insurance business in the United States is conducted by (life insurance companies / casualty insurance companies).

2. (Roughly half / A majority / Almost all) of Americans had some form of private (non-governmental) health insurance in 1997.

3. The most common form of health insurance is (individual insurance / association-sponsored group insurance / employer-sponsored group insurance).

4. The (property and casualty / life and health) sector of the insurance industry has more employees.

Types of Organizations (Page 10)

5. In addition to insurance companies, what are five other types of entities that provide protection against illness and injury?

Stock and Mutual Companies (Pages 10–15)

6. What are the two kinds of commercial insurance companies?

7. A large majority of commercial insurance companies are (stock companies / mutual companies).

8. The life insurance business in the United States is divided between mutual and stock companies in the following way: (stock companies have a majority of the business / mutual companies have a majority of the business / stock and mutual companies each have about half the business).

9. What distinguishes a stock company from another kind of company?

10. Who owns and controls a stock company?

11. What is the purpose of a stock insurance company?

12. How are votes distributed in stock companies?

13. How are a stock company's profits distributed?

14. When a new stock insurance company is formed, state regulations require that it have minimum amounts of money in what two areas?

♦ 15. Match these terms with the definitions below: **capital, dividend, liability,** and **surplus**.

  a. The money needed to start a business.

  b. The amount by which the value of an insurer's assets exceeds its liabilities.

  c. The probable cost of meeting a financial obligation.

  d. Periodic payment to stockholders of stock company profits.

16. Who owns and controls a mutual insurance company?

17. The purpose of a mutual insurer (is / is not) to make a profit and pay dividends.

18. How are votes distributed in mutual insurance companies?

19. Mutual insurers charge in premiums (only enough to cover costs / enough to cover costs and make a profit / enough to cover costs and add to a surplus).

20. What are the two purposes of a mutual company's surplus?

21. Under what circumstances would a mutual company pay dividends?

22. When a new mutual insurance company is formed, state regulations require that it meet minimums in two areas. What are they?

23. It is generally easier to form a new (mutual / stock) insurance company.

24. Almost all mutual insurers that now exist were organized originally as (mutual / stock) companies.

25. An insurance company can change its ownership (only from a stock company to a mutual company / only from a mutual company to a stock company / from a stock insurance company to a mutual insurance company and vice versa).

26. The process of ownership change (requires only the filing of a few legal documents and is usually relatively quick and simple / is subject to many legal and regulatory requirements and can be lengthy and expensive).

♦ 27. What is **demutualization**?

♦ 28. What is **mutualization**?

29. (Mutualization / Demutualization) is more common.

30. Why does a stock company have a greater ability to raise capital than a mutual company?

31. Compared to a stock company, a mutual company is limited in its ability to acquire other companies. What are three reasons why?

32. What advantage do stock companies have in attracting top-level employees?

33. Recent changes in the corporate income tax structure have placed a potentially higher tax burden on (mutual / stock) insurance companies.

34. What are three disadvantages of demutualization?

35. What is the main advantage of mutualization?

36. How is mutualization usually accomplished?

Other Organizations Providing Protection
(Pages 15–18)

37. Historically, how were Blue Cross and Blue Shield plans different from insurers?

38. What does it mean to say that the Blues were pre-paid service plans?

39. What have Blue Cross/Blue Shield plans and insurers always had in common?

40. Historically, what was the difference between Blue Cross and Blue Shield organizations?

41. Recently, Blue Cross/Blue Shield organizations have evolved to become (more / less) like insurers.

42. What are two advantages that Blue Cross/Blue Shield organizations historically enjoyed over insurers?

43. Historically, the Blues were expected to serve the community in a way insurance companies were not. What obligations did Blue Cross/Blue Shield organizations have that insurers did not?

◆ 44. What is **community rating**?

45. Blue Cross/Blue Shield plans currently (have / do not have) an exemption from federal income tax.

46. Many Blue Cross/Blue Shield plans are now (stock companies / mutual companies / both).

47. There are now (fewer / more) Blue Cross/Blue Shield plans than there were a decade ago.

48. What advantage does the Blue Cross and Blue Shield Association give Blue Cross and Blue Shield plans?

49. What are the three main powers that the Blue Cross and Blue Shield Association has over individual Blue Cross/Blue Shield plans?

50. What are three types of managed care organizations (MCOs)?

51. In recent years, the difference between managed care and health insurance has become (blurred / more distinct).

52. How did early types of MCOs, such as staff-model and group-model HMOs, operate?

53. What are two ways in which some MCOs have become more like insurance companies?

54. How have insurance companies become more like MCOs?

♦ 55. How does **self-insurance** work?

56. The number of self-insured groups is (growing / declining).

57. What are three advantages that self-insurance gives a company in providing health insurance to its employees?

58. Self-insured groups do not purchase insurance; (therefore, insurance companies have no involvement with them / however, insurance companies are involved with them).

♦ 59. How does an **administrative services only (ASO)** arrangement work?

♦ 60. How does a **minimum premium plan (MPP)** work?

♦ 61. In what two ways do **fraternal societies** differ from businesses?

62. Fraternal societies (are / are not) a major part of the insurance industry.

63. What is the purpose of laws governing fraternal societies that offer insurance?

64. (Medicare / Medicaid) serves persons over age 65 and others with certain disabilities.

65. (Medicare / Medicaid) serves a portion of the indigent population as well as certain categories of the medically needy.

♦ 66. What is the purpose of state **workers' compensation** programs?

67. Military programs provide health care benefits to (active members of the armed forces only / active service persons, veterans, and dependents).

The Canadian Life and Health Insurance Industry
(Pages 18–20)

68. Canadians rely on government programs to pay for most medical expenses, (so health insurance is not a major business in Canada / but health insurance is nevertheless a major business in Canada).

69. What are three of the private health care coverages common in Canada?

70. In Canada, more (life insurance companies / casualty insurance companies) offer health insurance.

71. What is the major factor that makes the Canadian insurance industry different from the U.S. insurance industry?

72. Canada has a (higher / lower) proportion of mutual insurance companies than the United States.

73. In Canada, (each province / the federal government) provides all residents with a comprehensive program of hospitalization and medical expense coverage.

74. What are the three main sources for funding of Canadian government health plans?

75. How does private health insurance fit into this government-sponsored program?

76. Why has the Canadian government encouraged stock companies to mutualize?

77. The Canadian government's pro-mutualization policy (has / has not) been a success.

78. The (Canadian / U.S.) government regulates the insurance industry more heavily.

79. In the United States, the regulation of insurance is primarily the responsibility of (the federal government / the states).

80. In Canada, the regulation of insurance is the responsibility of (the federal government / the provincial governments / both).

81. In Canada, the provinces have the sole responsibility for legislation in three main areas. What are they?

82. Under what conditions must an insurer have a provincial license?

83. Under what conditions must an insurer have a federal license?

84. In Canada (except in Nova Scotia), an insurer that has a federal license (must have / does not necessarily need) a provincial license.

85. In Canada (except in Nova Scotia), an insurer that has a provincial license (must have / does not necessarily need) a federal license.

86. Many Canadian companies that have no obligation to get a federal license voluntarily do so. Why?

87. How are inspection responsibilities divided between the federal and provincial governments in Canada?

Practice Exam Questions

1. Who owns a mutual insurance company?

    a. A fraternal society.

    b. The employees.

    c. The policyholders.

    d. The stockholders.

2. What would the management of a stock insurance company gain by converting to a mutual company?

    a. Easier access to capital.

    b. Greater ability to attract top executives.

    c. Greater ability to buy other companies.

    d. More control over the operations of the company.

3. In which of these areas have insurance companies traditionally had an advantage over Blue Cross / Blue Shield plans?

   a. Arrangements with physicians and hospitals.

   b. Community rating requirements.

   c. National marketing.

   d. Tax status.

4. What is the main role of private health insurance in Canada?

   a. Covers Canadians when they travel abroad.

   b. Provides coverage for retirees.

   c. Provides medical expense insurance.

   d. Supplements government coverage.

Answers

1. Life insurance companies.

2. A majority (70 percent).

3. Employer-sponsored group insurance.

4. Life and health.

5. Blue Cross/Blue Shield plans, managed care organizations, self-insured groups, fraternal societies, and government programs.

6. Stock companies and mutual companies.

7. Stock companies (93 percent).

8. Each type has about half.

9. People may purchase shares of the ownership of the company (shares of the company's stock).

10. The stockholders.

11. To earn money for its stockholders by selling insurance.

12. Each stockholder has one vote for every share of stock she owns.

13. Each stockholder receives a part of the profits in proportion to the number of shares he owns.

14. Capital and surplus funds.

15. a. Capital.

   b. Surplus.

   c. Liability.

   d. Dividend.

16. The policyholders.

17. Is not.

18. Each policyholder has one vote, regardless of the number of policies owned or the amount of insurance purchased.

19. Enough to cover costs and add to a surplus.

20. It serves as a margin of safety, a guarantee of the solvency and continuity of the organization despite any conceivable adverse circumstances; and it is used to cover new obligations that are assumed when new policies are sold.

21. If a company's surplus has reached its optimum size, excess amounts may be returned to the company's policyholders as dividends.

22. The number of applications for insurance accompanied by premiums and the amount of surplus funds.

23. Stock.

24. Stock.

25. From a stock insurance company to a mutual insurance company and vice versa.

26. Is subject to many legal and regulatory requirements and can be lengthy and expensive.

27. The change from mutual to stock ownership.

28. The change from stock to mutual ownership.

29. Demutualization.

30. Stock companies can raise money by selling new shares of stock.

31. • A mutual company cannot raise the money needed for acquisitions by issuing stock.

    • Regulations limit the ways mutual companies can use their surplus.

    • If a mutual company buys a stock company, the purchased company is subject to mutual regulations.

32. Stock companies can offer shares of company stock or stock options as part of the overall compensation package.

33. Mutual.

34. • The cost of accomplishing such a conversion;

    • the difficulty in making an equitable distribution of the mutual company's surplus among its policyholders; and

    • the complications in the process due to the great variation in applicable laws from state to state.

35. It gives the company's management more control over the operations of the company by freeing it from the demands of the stockholders.

36. By using surplus funds to buy all stock from the shareholders.

37. They were non-profit organizations, and they were pre-paid service plans, not insurance companies.

38. Subscribers of the Blues did not receive indemnification (compensation) to pay for medical expenses that they incurred; rather, in return for making monthly payments, they received certain specified medical services when they needed them directly from physicians or hospitals that were members of the plans.

39. They both have filled the same function of offering protection against the financial risk of illness or accident.

40. Blue Cross plans were sponsored by local hospital groups, and Blue Shield plans were sponsored by physician groups.

41. More.

42. Favorable reimbursement agreements with hospitals and doctors and preferential tax status.

43. Blues often had to accept as members people whom commercial insurers would not accept, and Blues were often required to practice community rating.

44. Charging everyone in the community the same rate, even if the characteristics of certain individuals or groups make them greater risks.

45. Do not have.

46. Both.

47. Fewer.

48. The association markets the plans on a national level, contracting with large national employer groups and the federal government on behalf of the local plans.

49. • The association can require the participation and cooperation of the local plans in contracts that it negotiates.

    • The association licenses the local plans to use the Blue Cross and Blue Shield names and symbols.

    • The association requires compliance with certain standards of organization, operations, products, and services.

50. Health maintenance organizations (HMOs), preferred provider organizations (PPOs), and point-of-service (POS) plans. (There are also other types.)

51. Blurred.

52. They did not compensate their members for the cost of medical care—rather they provided that care through physicians employed in the HMO's own facilities or through the HMO's network of contracted physicians. They did not compensate for any care provided outside their facilities or networks.

53. • Many new types of MCOs give their members more freedom in choosing their health care providers.

    • While early MCOs were typically not-for-profit organizations, many MCOs are now for-profit businesses, and some are owned by insurance companies and Blue Cross/ Blue Shield plans.

54. They have adopted techniques developed by MCOs to improve the quality and cost-effectiveness of health care.

55. A large company or union, instead of purchasing coverage for its employees or members from an insurer, establishes its own health insurance program and pays claims out of its own funds.

56. Growing.

57. The company can cut out the middleman, improve cash flow, and enjoy tax and regulatory advantages.

58. Insurance companies are involved with them.

59. Insurers process claims and provide other administrative services to a self-insured group in return for a fee.

60. An employer takes responsibility for the group's expected level of claims and purchases insurance to cover claims above this expected level.

61. Although they offer insurance, they are primarily social organizations; they provide insurance only to their own members.

62. Are not.

63. To ensure that the organization has the financial capacity to meet all of its insurance commitments.

64. Medicare.

65. Medicaid.

66. They pay benefits to those suffering from work-related injuries and diseases.

67. Active service persons, veterans, and dependents.

68. Health insurance is a major business in Canada.

69. Extended health care insurance, dental insurance, and long-term disability insurance.

70. Life insurance companies.

71. In Canada, a government-administered health care system dominates the health care field, whereas the United States does not have such a system.

72. Higher.

73. Each province.

74. Grants from provincial and federal governments, direct or general tax revenues, and premiums paid by users of the plans.

75. It is available and may be used to meet needs not met by government coverage.

76. The Canadian government has been concerned about Canadian companies being taken over by foreign companies. Since mutual companies do not have stock that foreign companies can buy, they are much more difficult to acquire than stock companies.

77. Has.

78. The U.S. (The Canadian system is highly self-regulated.)

79. The states.

80. Both.

81. The form of the insurance contract; advertising and consumer protection; and the licensing and regulation of agents, brokers, and adjusters.

82. All insurers must be licensed by every province in which they operate (except Nova Scotia).

83. All federally incorporated Canadian insurers and all non-Canadian insurers doing business in Canada must have a federal license in addition to their provincial license or licenses.

84. Must have.

85. Does not necessarily need.

86. For prestige.

87. The federal government inspects insurance companies licensed by it, and the provinces inspect insurers that are not also registered with the federal government.

Answers to Practice Exam Questions

1. c
2. d
3. b
4. d

3 MEDICAL EXPENSE COVERAGE

Introduction (Page 21)

1. Medical expense coverage protects the insured against financial losses due to illness or injury by (paying a lump sum / making monthly payments / reimbursing for expenses).

2. What are the two major types of medical expense coverage?

3. What are the two types of major medical insurance?

4. Hospital-surgical insurance, supplemental major medical insurance, and comprehensive major medical insurance are offered on a (group / individual / both group and individual) basis.

Hospital-Surgical Insurance (Pages 21–25)

5. Hospital-surgical insurance and basic medical expense insurance are (different coverages / two names for the same thing).

6. In what two ways are various hospital-surgical policies different from each other?

7. Under which category of hospital-surgical benefits do the following expenses fall? (The categories are: hospital room and board charges, miscellaneous hospital charges, surgical charges, physician's inhospital charges, and charges for outpatient services.)

   a. Operating room expenses.

   b. Fees charged by a surgeon for inhospital surgical operations.

   c. Inhospital services of pathologists, radiologists, and anesthetists.

   d. Fees charged by a physician for nonsurgical treatment during hospital confinement.

   e. General nursing care.

   f. Laboratory services furnished during a hospital stay.

   g. Outpatient lab services.

   h. Fees charged by a surgeon for outpatient surgical operations.

   i. Ambulance service.

   j. X-ray examinations performed during a hospital stay.

   k. Outpatient diagnostic X-ray services.

   l. Medicines, drugs, and surgical dressings furnished during a hospital stay.

8. The amount of benefits paid for an expense by a hospital-surgical policy is determined in one of two ways. What are these two ways?

9. The amount paid by hospital-surgical policies for hospital room and board is now usually (a preset daily maximum / whatever the hospital charges for a semi-private room).

10. For policies that pay a daily maximum for hospital room and board, the amount differs from policy to policy. What is the main factor in the difference?

11. Surgical schedules of hospital-surgical policies limit benefits for common surgical procedures in either of two ways. What are these two ways?

12. Bill has a hospital-surgical policy that requires a second surgical opinion for optional surgery, but Bill has optional surgery without seeking a second opinion. What will the insurer probably do?

13. Hospital-surgical policies usually limit benefits for physicians' inhospital charges by (setting a maximum payment amount for each physician visit / limiting the number of visits / either / both).

14. Hospital-surgical policies limit benefits for outpatient diagnostic X-ray and lab charges in either of two ways. What are these two ways?

15. Hospital-surgical policies (may make maternity coverage optional or cover only part of maternity expenses / must cover maternity in full just like any other illness or health condition / either, depending on the state).

♦ 16. What does an **exclusion** state?

♦ 17. What does a **limitation** state?

♦ 18. What is a **preexisting condition**?

♦ 19. What is a **look-back period**?

20. Why do medical expense policies commonly exclude or limit payment for preexisting conditions?

21. The look-back period of a typical group medical expense policy is (three or six / six or nine / nine or twelve) months.

22. Tom became covered by his employer's group medical expense policy in December. The policy has a look-back period of six months. Tom was treated for diabetes the previous January but was not treated for it since that time. Would the policy exclude diabetes as a preexisting condition?

23. What if Tom was treated in October?

24. Once a preexisting condition has been identified, the insurer (never / sometimes) pays benefits for it.

25. Preexisting conditions are treated differently in individual medical expense policies than in group policies. What are the two main differences?

♦ 26. What does **HIPAA** stand for?

27. The use of exclusions for preexisting conditions are restricted by (federal laws only / state laws only / both federal and state laws).

28. HIPAA imposes restrictions on the use of exclusions for preexisting conditions in group policies. What are the restrictions in each of these areas?

    a. Pregnancy.

    b. The look-back period.

    c. The period during which benefits are not paid for a preexisting condition.

    d. Persons moving from one group plan to another.

29. Marianne worked for Hexagon Corporation for eight months, during which time she was covered by Hexagon's group medical expense insurance. She left Hexagon and a month later was hired by Polymer, Inc. She began coverage under Polymer's group medical expense insurance her first day of work. If she had a preexisting condition, for how long could this condition be excluded by the new insurer?

30. If during her job change Marianne had gone for three months without coverage, how long could the condition be excluded?

31. If Marianne's preexisting condition was pregnancy, how long could it be excluded?

32. Bart was also recently hired by Polymer. He had been insured under his previous health plan for two years, and the gap between coverages was one month. If he had a preexisting condition, how long could this condition be excluded?

33. Margaret also began working at Polymer. She has never previously had health insurance coverage. If she had a preexisting condition, how long could it be excluded?

34. Why is each of the following often subject to exclusions or limitations?

    a. Intentionally self-inflicted injuries.

    b. Dental care, vision care and eyeglasses, and hearing aids.

    c. Custodial care (long-term nursing care).

    d. Occupational accidents and sicknesses.

    e. Care received from any government agency.

    f. Military service and war.

◆ 35. What are **elective medical services**?

36. Routine health examinations or periodic check-ups (may / may not) be classified as elective medical services.

Major Medical Insurance (Pages 25–28)

37. The most common form of medical expense insurance is now by far (surgical-hospital insurance / major medical insurance).

38. What are the two principal differences between major medical policies and hospital-surgical policies?

39. Eileen has a medical expense policy that does not require her to pay any deductibles or coinsurance, but she does sometimes have to pay for medical expenses that the policy does not cover. Eileen probably has a (hospital-surgical / major medical) policy.

40. Gary has a medical expense policy that requires him to pay a deductible and coinsurance, but he rarely has to pay for medical expenses not covered by the policy. Gary probably has a (hospital-surgical / major medical) policy.

41. What are the two kinds of major medical insurance?

42. What is the difference between supplemental and comprehensive major medical?

43. (Supplemental / Comprehensive) major medical has the advantage of simplicity of plan design and the avoidance of overlapping coverages.

44. (Supplemental / Comprehensive) is more common.

45. How does supplemental major medical insurance differ from the forms of insurance usually referred to as supplemental coverages (or supplemental insurance)?

46. Major medical policies (have / do not have) exclusions and limitations.

♦ 47. What is a **deductible**?

♦ 48. What does it mean to say a deductible is **cumulative**?

♦ 49. What is an **accumulation period** for a deductible?

50. What happens when an accumulation period is over?

51. What is the normal accumulation period?

♦ 52. What is **first-dollar coverage**?

53. Jill has a major medical policy with a $500 annual deductible. She incurs covered medical expenses of $1,375. How much will Jill pay and how much will the insurer pay?

54. Pat also has a major medical policy with a $500 annual deductible. He incurs covered medical expenses of $350. How much will Pat pay and how much will the insurer pay?

55. Later, Pat incurs another expense of $600. How much will Pat pay and how much will the insurer pay?

56. Still later, Pat incurs a third expense of $750. How much will Pat pay and how much will the insurer pay?

57. Several months later Pat incurs a fourth expense of $800. However, it is now a new calendar year and a new deductible is in effect. How much will Pat pay and how much will the insurer pay?

58. What is the maximum amount Pat could pay in deductible payments during a single calendar year?

59. What are the two purposes of the deductible?

60. What is the advantage to the insured of a deductible?

◆ 61. Which does each of these sentences describe, an **all cause deductible** or a **per cause deductible**?

    a. All expenses incurred for all illnesses and accidents apply to one deductible.

    b. There is a separate deductible for each illness or accident.

    c. The accumulation period is almost universally the calendar year.

    d. The accumulation period for each cause starts on the date of the first expense for that cause and normally ends one or two years later.

    e. This deductible has the advantages of being simple to administer and easy for the insured to understand.

    f. This deductible is much more common.

62. Rick has a major medical policy with a per cause deductible. He is in an automobile accident and begins incurring expenses. One year later the accumulation period of the deductible ends, but Rick is still incurring expenses. What happens?

63. What are the two types of deductibles that are used by supplemental major medical plans to coordinate benefits with the basic plans that they supplement?

64. The (integrated deductible / corridor deductible) is more common.

65. The amount of the (integrated deductible / corridor deductible) is usually greater.

66. Kevin has hospital-surgical insurance and a supplemental major medical plan with a $500 corridor deductible. He incurs $2,000 in medical expenses. His hospital-surgical policy pays $800 of these expenses. How much will Kevin pay and how much will his major medical pay?

67. As above, Kevin has a supplemental major medical plan with a $500 corridor deductible and he incurs $2,000 in medical expenses. But now suppose his hospital-surgical policy pays $300 of these expenses. How much will Kevin pay and how much will his major medical pay?

68. Now let us suppose that instead of a corridor deductible, Kevin's supplemental major medical plan has a $1,000 *integrated* deductible. As before, Kevin incurs $2000 in medical expenses and his hospital-surgical policy pays $800 of these expenses. How much will Kevin pay and how much will his major medical pay?

69. As above, Kevin's major medical has a $1,000 integrated deductible, but this time suppose that of the total $2,000 in expenses his hospital-surgical insurance pays $300. How much will Kevin pay and how much will his major medical pay?

70. Finally, as above, Kevin's major medical has a $1,000 integrated deductible, but now

suppose that of the total $2,000 in expenses his hospital-surgical insurance pays $1,200. How much will Kevin pay and how much will his major medical pay?

◆ 71. How does a **family deductible** work?

72. What is the amount of a family deductible compared to a standard deductible?

◆ 73. What is **coinsurance**?

74. What is the purpose of coinsurance?

75. How do some plans limit the amount an insured can pay in coinsurance?

76. Steven has a major medical policy with a deductible of $500 and 20 percent coinsurance. He incurs medical expenses of $800. Assuming this is Steven's first expense of this deductible accumulation period, how much will Steven pay and how much will his insurer pay?

◆ 77. What is an **overall maximum benefit**?

78. What are the two kinds of overall maximum benefits?

Practice Exam Questions

1. Which of these does the Health Insurance Portability and Accountability Act (HIPAA) prohibit group policies from excluding as a preexisting condition?

   a. HIV/AIDS.

   b. Mental/behavioral conditions.

   c. Occupational illnesses or injuries.

   d. Pregnancy.

2. Hospital-surgical plans

   a. are more common than major medical plans.

   b. typically have coinsurance.

   c. typically have deductibles.

   d. usually provide less coverage than major medical plans.

3. The per cause deductible, compared to the all cause deductible,

   a. is easier for the insured to understand.

   b. is more common.

   c. is simpler to administer.

   d. sometimes has a longer accumulation period.

4. The deductible most commonly used in supplemental major medical policies to coordinate benefits with the basic plans they supplement is the

   a. all cause deductible.

   b. corridor deductible.

   c. integrated deductible.

   d. per cause deductible.

Answers

1. Reimbursing for expenses.

2. Hospital-surgical insurance and major medical insurance.

3. Comprehensive and supplemental.

4. Both group and individual.

5. Two names for the same thing.

6. In the expenses they cover and in the amount they pay for a given expense.

7. a. Miscellaneous hospital charges.

    b. Surgical charges.

    c. Miscellaneous hospital charges.

    d. Physician's inhospital charges.

    e. Hospital room and board charges.

    f. Miscellaneous hospital charges.

    g. Charges for outpatient services.

    h. Surgical charges.

    i. Miscellaneous hospital charges.

    j. Miscellaneous hospital charges.

    k. Charges for outpatient services.

    l. Miscellaneous hospital charges.

8. Establishing an amount in advance or basing benefits on usual and customary charges.

9. Whatever the hospital charges for a semi-private room.

10. Geography.

11. The schedule establishes a set amount, or the amount is a percentage of the overall policy maximum.

12. Refuse to pay anything or pay less than normal.

13. Both.

14. Setting maximum amounts payable for any one illness or injury, or setting overall maximum benefits.

15. Either, depending on the state.

16. What expenses the insurer will not reimburse and under what circumstances it will not pay benefits for expenses that would usually be reimbursed.

17. For what expenses and under what circumstances the insurer will pay benefits but at a reduced level.

18. A medical condition that an insured had before her insurance policy went into effect.

19. Most group medical expense policies only exclude preexisting conditions that the insured has been treated for during a certain period of time before the policy takes effect. This period is known as the look-back period.

20. Without uncertainty insurance does not make economic sense, either for the insurer or the insured. If the insurer knows with certainty that a potential insured will incur certain expenses, in order to offer coverage it would have to charge the insured as a premium the full cost of those expenses plus administrative

costs. Neither the insured nor the insurer would gain anything by the arrangement.

21. Three or six.

22. No, it was not treated during the six-month look-back period.

23. Yes, this treatment falls within the six-month look-back period.

24. Sometimes. (Under some group policies, once someone has been insured for a certain period of time or meets other criteria, preexisting conditions are covered on the same basis as any other condition.)

25. In individual coverage, look-back periods can be as long as three years and exclusions may last longer.

26. The federal Health Insurance Portability and Accountability Act of 1996.

27. Both federal and state laws.

28. a. It cannot be treated as a preexisting condition.

    b. It cannot be more than six months.

    c. It cannot be more than 12 months.

    d. In this case, the 12-month period is reduced by the amount of time the person was covered by the previous plan (provided the gap between coverage under the two plans is not greater than 63 days).

29. Four months. (The 12-month maximum period established by HIPAA minus the eight months of previous group coverage.)

30. 12 months. The gap between coverage would be more than 63 days, so the 12-month maximum would not be not reduced.

31. Under HIPAA pregnancy cannot be treated as a preexisting condition.

32. It could not be excluded for any period of time. The period of exclusion is 12 months minus the amount of time the insured was previously insured. In Bart's case this is 12 months minus two years, or zero.

33. 12 months. 12 months minus the amount of time she was previously insured (zero months) is 12 months.

34. a. The principle of uncertainty requires that the insured not collect benefits from hazards that he directly causes himself.

    b. Covered by various supplemental insurance policies.

    c. Provided by long-term care insurance.

    d. Covered by state workers' compensation programs.

    e. The insured does not actually pay for these services, so he does not need to be reimbursed for their cost.

    f. This exclusion is intended to prevent the insurer from making promises it cannot keep. If a war occurs there would be so many claims that the insurer would not have the resources to pay them all.

35. Services not necessary to alleviate illness or injury, such as cosmetic surgery or treatment for sexual dysfunction.

36. May.

37. Major medical insurance.

38. Major medical generally provides much greater coverage; hospital-surgical plans do not have deductibles and coinsurance, while major medical plans do.

39. Hospital-surgical.

40. Major medical.

41. Supplemental major medical and comprehensive major medical.

42. Supplemental provides coverage for expenses not covered by a basic (hospital-surgical) plan and adds additional benefits for those expenses that are covered but in a limited way; comprehensive combines in one plan all the coverage provided by a hospital-surgical plan and a supplemental major medical plan.

43. Comprehensive.

44. Comprehensive.

45. Supplemental coverages supplement a broad-based plan of medical expense insurance that provides coverage for most necessary medical expenses. Supplemental major medical insurance, on the other hand, is combined with basic hospital-surgical coverage to form such a broad-based plan.

46. Have.

47. The amount of covered expense that must be incurred and paid by the insured before benefits become payable by the insurer.

48. The deductible does not have to be satisfied every time the insured incurs an expense; rather each expense is added until the deductible is satisfied, after which all expenses are covered by the insurer.

49. The period of time during which incurred expenses count toward satisfying the deductible.

50. The insured must begin to satisfy a new deductible.

51. The calendar year (January 1 to December 31).

52. If a coverage does not require a deductible, it is said to offer first-dollar coverage—that is, it pays benefits beginning with the first dollar of covered expense.

53. Jill will pay $500 and the insurer will pay $875.

54. Pat will pay $350 and the insurer will pay nothing.

55. Pat will pay $150 (the remainder of the deductible) and the insurer will pay $450.

56. Pat will pay nothing and the insurer will pay $750 because the deductible has already been satisfied.

57. Pat will pay $500 (to satisfy the new deductible) and the insurer will pay the rest.

58. $500.

59. It discourages the insured from unnecessarily incurring costs (since she will have to pay a portion of these costs), and it eliminates small claims and the expense of handling them.

60. It allows the insurer to keep costs and the price of premiums down.

61. a. All cause deductible.

    b. Per cause deductible.

    c. All cause deductible.

    d. Per cause deductible.

    e. All cause deductible.

    f. All cause deductible.

62. Rick must satisfy a new deductible, and a new accumulation period begins.

63. Corridor deductible and integrated deductible.

64. Corridor deductible.

65. Integrated deductible.

66. Kevin pays $500 and his major medical pays $700. Major medical pays for the total expenses minus what the hospital-surgical policy pays, minus the deductible, which Kevin pays.

    $2,000 (total expenses)
    – $800 (minus amount paid by hospital-surgical policy)
    – $500 (minus amount of deductible paid by Kevin)
    $700 (remainder paid by major medical)

67. Kevin still pays $500; his major medical pays $1,200. Major medical again pays for the total expenses minus what the hospital-surgical policy pays, minus the deductible, which Kevin pays. Kevin always pays the same—the amount of the deductible (until that deductible is satisfied).

    $2,000 (total expenses)
    – $300 (minus amount paid by hospital-surgical policy)
    – $500 (minus amount of deductible paid by Kevin)
    $1,200 (remainder paid by major medical)

68. Kevin pays $200 and his major medical pays $1,000. Major medical pays expenses over $1,000, regardless of how much or how little the hospital-surgical policy pays. Kevin must always make up the difference between what the hospital-surgical coverage pays and $1,000.

69. Kevin pays $700. To repeat, Kevin must always make up the difference between what the hospital-surgical coverage pays and $1,000.

70. Kevin pays nothing. Since the payment by the hospital-surgical plan exceeds the $1,000 deductible amount, there is no difference that Kevin has to make up. Kevin's major medical pays $800.

71. A family deductible applies to an entire family. It can be satisfied by expenses incurred by any member of the family, and once it is satisfied, it is satisfied for all family members.

72. Two, two-and-a-half, or three times the standard deductible.

73. The arrangement by which the insurer and the insured each pay a percentage of covered losses after the deductible is met.

74. To discourage the insured from using medical services unnecessarily by having her pay a portion of the expense of any service.

75. Many plans apply a dollar limit (for example, $1,000) to the coinsurance to be borne by the insured during any one calendar year.

76. Steven will pay $560—the $500 deductible and 20 percent of the remaining $300, or $60.

77. The maximum amount of money that the insurer has the obligation to pay.

78. Lifetime (all cause) or per cause.

Answers to Practice Exam Questions

1. d

2. d

3. d

4. b

4 SUPPLEMENTAL COVERAGES

Introduction (Page 29)

1. What are the three main ways supplemental coverages supplement other coverages?

Dental Insurance (Pages 29–32)

◆ 2. What is an **integrated dental plan**?

◆ 3. What is a **non-integrated dental plan**?

◆ 4. A **stand-alone dental plan** and a non-integrated dental plan are (different / two terms for the same thing).

◆ 5. What is **scheduled reimbursement** based on?

◆ 6. What is **nonscheduled reimbursement** based on?

7. Generally, integrated plans reimburse on a (nonscheduled basis / scheduled basis / either).

8. Generally, non-integrated plans reimburse on a (nonscheduled basis / scheduled basis / either).

9. To what class of dental services does each of these services belong? (The classes are: diagnostic, preventive, restorative, prosthodontics, oral surgery, periodontics or endodontics, and orthodontics.)

   a. Straightening treatment.

   b. Installment and maintenance of bridgework.

   c. Fillings, inlays, and crowns.

   d. Treatment of gums.

10. What class of dental service is by far the most common?

11. The accumulation period of a dental plan deductible is usually (six months / the calendar year).

12. Most integrated dental plans have (a single deductible / separate deductibles) for dental and medical expenses.

13. Why is a dental deductible usually not applied to preventive and diagnostic services?

14. Most dental plans have (different / the same) deductible amounts, coinsurance percentages, and maximum benefit amounts for different classes of dental services.

15. In dental plans, the percentage of coinsurance is usually (less / greater) for major procedures than for basic procedures.

16. How do some nonintegrated dental plans limit benefits?

17. What are three common limitations and exclusions of dental policies?

18. Why are orthodontic services often optional?

Prescription Drug Insurance (Pages 32–33)

19. Most prescription drug insurance plans are (individual / group) policies.

◆ 20. What is a **copayment**?

21. How does a copayment differ from coinsurance?

22. Jason is covered by a prescription drug plan with a $10 copayment. He has a prescription filled that costs $30. How much does Jason pay?

23. If the prescription costs $75, how much does Jason pay?

24. The copayment for generic drugs is usually (lower / higher).

25. What are the two types of prescription drug plans?

◆ 26. Leanne buys drugs from a pharmacist and then submits a claim form to her insurer. Leanne has a (**reimbursement plan / service plan**).

◆ 27. Betsy gets drugs from a pharmacist and pays him a copayment. Her insurer reimburses the pharmacist. Betsy does not have to make a claim. Betsy has a (**reimbursement plan / service plan**).

28. Carol can get drugs from any pharmacist. She has a (reimbursement plan / service plan).

29. Dennis must get drugs from a pharmacist who participates in his plan. He has a (reimbursement plan / service plan).

30. In a reimbursement plan, benefits are usually based on (a schedule / usual and customary charges).

31. What disadvantages do service plans have for an insurer?

32. Why do third-party administrators generally manage service plans for insurance companies?

33. Mail-order prescription drug programs are (reimbursement plans / service plans).

34. Whom do mail-order prescription drug programs serve?

35. Why does prescription drug insurance usually exclude drugs that are dispensed while the individual is confined in a hospital or extended care facility?

36. How are contraceptive drugs or medicines normally treated by prescription drug insurance?

37. How do prescription drug policies limit prescriptions?

38. What products are usually excluded in prescription drug policies?

Vision Care Insurance (Pages 33–34)

39. Vision care insurance is usually offered on a (group / individual) basis.

40. Of the following services, which are normally reimbursed by vision care insurance, which are normally excluded, and what limitations apply?

    a. Eye examinations.

    b. Medical or surgical treatment.

    c. Single vision lenses.

    d. Tinted lenses.

    e. Bifocal and trifocal lenses.

    f. Contact lenses.

    g. Sunglasses.

    h. Safety glasses.

    i. Duplication of lenses due to breakage or loss.

    j. Frames.

41. Most vision care programs require that services be authorized by a professional. What professional?

42. What are the three ways in which vision plans reimburse insureds?

Hospital Indemnity Insurance (Page 34)

43. Hospital indemnity benefits are (a flat dollar amount for each day, week, or month the insured is confined in a hospital / based on actual expenses incurred by the insured).

44. Hospital indemnity benefits are (coordinated with other benefits the insured may receive to avoid duplication / paid in addition to and regardless of any other benefits the insured may receive).

45. Hospital indemnity benefits are paid (from the first day of hospital confinement / after a waiting period of 30 days).

46. Hospital indemnity benefits are paid for (a sickness only / either a sickness or an injury).

47. How are hospital indemnity benefits usually limited?

48. Hospital indemnity insurance is usually offered as an optional supplement to what coverage?

49. What are the three kinds of expenses for which hospital indemnity insurance is intended to provide money?

50. What is meant by out-of-pocket payments required by other coverages?

51. What are some of the medical expenses that might not be covered by other insurance policies?

52. What are some of the incidental expenses that might be incurred during an illness.

Critical Illness Insurance (Page 35)

53. What are the three ways in which critical illness insurance is like hospital indemnity insurance?

54. What is the main difference between critical illness insurance and hospital indemnity insurance?

55. A critical illness policy pays benefits (for any serious illness or injury / only for the serious illnesses and injuries specified in the policy).

56. What are some of the illnesses and injuries typically covered by critical illness insurance?

57. The lump sum paid by a critical illness policy is (the same for any covered illness or injury / different for different illnesses or injuries).

58. Critical illness insurance benefits are paid (from the first day of diagnosis / after a waiting period of 30 days after diagnosis).

59. Critical illness insurance is available (to all ages / only to persons age 18 through 64).

60. A critical illness policy pays a lump-sum benefit (only once / as often as a serious illness occurs).

61. Critical illness policies are sold (only as stand-alone policies / only as riders to other coverages / either).

Specified Disease Insurance (Pages 35–36)

62. How does specified disease insurance differ from critical illness insurance?

63. What disease is most commonly covered by specified disease insurance?

64. How is specified disease insurance like hospital indemnity insurance and critical illness insurance?

65. Why are incidental costs sometimes large for cancer patients and their families?

66. In which of the following ways do specified disease policies pay benefits? (A lump sum like critical illness insurance / reimbursement for expenses like medical expense insurance / a flat dollar amount per amount of time like hospital indemnity insurance).

Accidental Death and Dismemberment Insurance (AD&D)
(Pages 36–37)

✦ 67. What is a **principal sum** in the context of AD&D?

68. In terms of the principal sum of the policy, how much will an insurer probably pay for the following losses?

   a. Loss of life.

   b. Loss of one hand.

   c. Loss of one foot.

   d. Loss of one eye.

   e. Loss of two feet in the same accident.

   f. Loss of one eye and one hand in the same accident.

   g. Loss of two feet and one eye in the same accident.

69. AD&D pays benefits (only for accidents / for accidents and illnesses).

70. Would AD&D coverage pay benefits in the following circumstances?

   a. Injury due to suicide attempt.

   b. Intentionally self-inflicted injury.

   c. Bacterial infection resulting from an accidental wound.

   d. Injury resulting from war.

   e. Injury resulting from illegal drug use.

   f. Injury resulting from the use of drugs prescribed by a physician.

✦ 71. What is the difference between **nonoccupational** and **24-hour AD&D**?

✦ 72. **Group life supplement** AD&D is a(n) (optional / non-optional) supplement to an employer's group life insurance.

✦ 73. **Voluntary AD&D** is (individual insurance / optional group insurance).

74. How is the principal sum of a group life supplement AD&D policy usually determined?

75. Group life supplement AD&D usually continues (as long as the life insurance policy it supplements / until retirement, even if the life insurance policy continues after retirement).

✦ 76. **Business trip AD&D** provides coverage for employees in what situation?

77. Business trip AD&D usually is paid (entirely by the employer / by both employer and employee).

78. How do the three types of business trip AD&D plans differ?

    a. Comprehensive (or all risk) plans.

    b. Common carrier plans.

    c. All conveyance plans.

♦ 79. What is a **common carrier**?

80. AD&D plans cover (only employees / employees and dependents / either).

Travel Accident Insurance (Page 38)

81. For what losses does travel accident insurance provide benefits?

82. What period does travel accident insurance usually cover?

83. What is the main difference between AD&D and travel accident insurance?

84. What are some of the ways travel accident insurance policies are sold?

85. What is the advantage of these sales methods?

Accident Medical Expense Insurance (Page 38)

86. What does accident medical expense insurance reimburse for?

87. How do accident medical expense insurance and regular medical expense insurance differ?

88. What are three common ways in which accident medical expense benefits are limited?

Medicare Supplement Insurance (Pages 38–41)

89. Since Medicare pays for health care for people age 65 and over, why do the elderly need Medicare supplement insurance?

90. Who receives Medicare Part A?

91. Beneficiaries (pay / do not pay) a portion of Medicare Part A premiums.

92. In the following cases the individuals are Medicare Part A beneficiaries. What portion of hospital charges must the individuals pay?

    a. Stella is hospitalized for 45 days.

    b. Harold is hospitalized for 70 days.

    c. Sarah is hospitalized for 180 days. Sarah has not used any of her lifetime benefit of 60 extra days of hospital care.

    d. Later, Sarah is again hospitalized. At what point will she have to begin paying for all hospital expenses?

93. A Medicare Part A beneficiary (can use some of the 60 extra days of hospital care during one hospital stay and some during other stays / can use the 60 days for one hospital stay only).

94. Edward, a Medicare Part A beneficiary, spends 35 days in the hospital and then enters a skilled nursing facility, where he stays for 200 days. What benefits will Medicare Part A pay and what will Edward pay?

95. If Edward has another period of illness, what benefits will he have?

96. Medicare Part A pays nursing facility benefits (only after the beneficiary has spent at least three days in a hospital / whether the beneficiary has been hospitalized or not).

97. What benefits does Medicare Part A provide in these areas?

    a. Home health services.

    b. Hospice benefits for terminally ill patients.

    c. Blood.

98. Participation in Medicare Part B is (automatic / voluntary) for Medicare beneficiaries.

99. Beneficiaries pay (0 / 10 / 25) percent of Medicare Part B premiums.

100. In which one of the following areas does Medicare Part B *not* pay benefits? Physicians' treatments, prescription drugs, surgical procedures, hospital outpatient services, and medical supplies.

101. If an elderly person receives both Medicare Part A and Part B, all his possible medical expenses (are / are not) covered.

102. The federal government requires all Medicare supplement policies to be standardized into ten plans labeled A through J. Insurance companies in this market (can offer only one of these plans / can offer up to three of these plans / can offer any of these plans / must offer Plan A and can offer any other plan).

103. According to Figure 4.2, which is the most popular Medicare supplement plan?

Practice Exam Questions

1. In most dental plans, the insured does not have to pay a deductible for
   I.   diagnostic services.
   II.   preventative services.
   III. restorative services.

   a. I and II only.

   b. I and III only.

   c. II and III only.

   d. I, II, and III.

2. Hospital indemnity benefits are based on

   a. a pre-set amount per day in the hospital.

   b. a pre-set lump-sum amount.

   c. actual hospital expenses incurred by the insured.

   d. reasonable and customary hospital charges.

3. Critical illness insurance pays benefits for

   a. any serious illness or injury.

   b. any serious illness, but not injuries.

   c. only illnesses and injuries specified in the policy.

   d. only one specified illness.

4. Beneficiaries of Medicare Part A do <u>not</u> pay

   a. copayments.

   b. deductibles.

   c. premiums.

   d. out-of-pocket expenses.

Answers

1. • By reimbursing for the portion of expenses that a medical expense policy requires the insured to pay (such as deductibles and coinsurance);

   • by paying benefits for the kinds of expenses that a medical expense policy may exclude (such as dental, prescription drug, and vision expenses); and

   • by covering the non-medical expenses that often result from a major illness (such as child care and travel and lodging for family members).

2. A dental plan that is part of a medical expense policy.

3. A dental plan that is not part of a medical expense policy, but is rather an entirely separate policy.

4. Two terms for the same thing.

5. A schedule that specifies amounts for given services.

6. The usual and customary charges for services.

7. Nonscheduled.

8. Either.

9. a. Orthodontics.

   b. Prosthodontics.

   c. Restorative.

   d. Periodontics or endodontics.

10. Restorative.

11. The calendar year.

12. A single deductible.

13. To encourage preventive care.

14. Different.

15. Greater.

16. They may have a calendar year or policy year maximum on benefits, a lifetime maximum for orthodontic benefits, and/or a lifetime maximum on periodontal care.

17. • The frequency of some services may be limited.

   • Cosmetic and experimental services are excluded.

   • Replacement of teeth missing prior to the effective date of the dental plan may be excluded entirely or covered at a reduced reimbursement rate.

18. They are expensive and including them in a policy can significantly increase premiums, so the insured is allowed to decide whether she wants to receive and pay extra premiums for these services.

19. Group.

20. A flat dollar amount that the insured pays each time a certain kind of service is received.

21. A copayment is not a percentage of the total cost, like coinsurance, but rather is always the same dollar amount even though the total cost of the service may vary.

22. $10.

23. $10. The copayment remains the same, no matter how much the prescription actually costs.

24. Lower.

25. Reimbursement and service.

26. Reimbursement plan.

27. Service plan.

28. Reimbursement plan.

29. Service plan.

30. Usual and customary charges.

31. They require extensive networks of participating pharmacies and involve a large number of small claims.

32. Their high volume of business allows them to minimize administrative costs and negotiate discounts with participating pharmacies.

33. Service plans.

34. Those who use maintenance medication and find it convenient to buy long-term supplies.

35. They are normally covered by regular medical expense insurance.

36. They are usually excluded, but may be covered at the policyholder's request for an additional premium.

37. They are usually limited to a specified number of days' supply of a drug.

38. Devices of any type (such as hypodermic needles or syringes), bandages, sexual dysfunction drugs, beauty aids or cosmetics, dietary supplements, immunization agents, sera, blood, and blood plasma.

39. Group.

40. a. Reimbursed, but usually limited to one examination per 12-month period.

    b. Excluded.

    c. Reimbursed, but usually limited to one pair per 12-month period.

    d. Excluded.

    e. Reimbursed, but usually limited to one pair per 12-month period.

    f. Reimbursed, but usually limited to one pair per 12-month period.

    g. Excluded.

    h. Excluded.

    i. Excluded.

    j. Reimbursed, but usually limited to one pair every two years. The cost is limited to the price of average frames.

41. An ophthalmologist or optometrist.

42. • Reimbursement for all expenses up to a flat dollar maximum per individual per calendar year;

    • reimbursement based on usual and customary charges; or

    • reimbursement based on a specified schedule.

43. A flat dollar amount.

44. Paid in addition to and regardless of any other benefits the insured may receive.

45. From the first day of hospital confinement.

46. Either a sickness or an injury.

47. By a maximum benefit period.

48. Medical expense insurance.

49. • Out-of-pocket payments required by other coverages;

    • medical expenses not covered by other insurance policies; and

• incidental expenses incurred during the illness.

50. Deductibles, coinsurance, copayments, and payments for expenses that exceed overall maximums.

51. Experimental treatments, additional medical opinions, additional prescription drugs, rehabilitation services, and home health care.

52. Child care, transportation, home or auto modification, housekeeping, and lost income of both the patient and family members who must take time off work.

53. Benefits are not based on actual expenses; they are paid in addition to and regardless of any other benefits the insured may receive; and they are intended to provide money for the insured to pay for out-of-pocket payments, medical expenses not paid by other coverage, and incidental expenses.

54. The benefit paid by hospital indemnity insurance is based on the amount of time the insured spends in the hospital; critical illness insurance pays a lump sum.

55. Only for illnesses and injuries specified in the policy.

56. Heart attack, angioplasty, heart bypass, major organ transplant, stroke, kidney failure, paralysis, cancer, Alzheimer's disease, multiple sclerosis, and the loss of sight, limb, hearing, or speech.

57. Different for different illnesses or injuries.

58. After a waiting period of 30 days after diagnosis.

59. Only to persons age 18 through 64.

60. Only once. (Coverage terminates after the lump sum is paid.)

61. Either.

62. Critical illness coverage pays benefits for a number of specified illness and injuries. Specified disease insurance pays benefits for *one* stipulated disease.

63. Cancer.

64. Specified disease insurance usually pays benefits in addition to those received from other insurance policies and so serves to provide the insured with money to pay for expenses not covered by his other insurance—out-of-pocket payments,

noncovered medical expenses, and incidental costs.

65. They may incur transportation, food, and lodging expenses when they travel to other cities for specialized care.

66. Reimbursement for expenses; flat amount per amount of time.

67. An amount established by an AD&D policy for the purpose of determining benefits. Benefits for different losses are defined as all or part of this amount.

68. a. All of the principal sum.

    b. One-half the principal sum.

    c. One-half the principal sum.

    d. One-half the principal sum.

    e. All of the principal sum.

    f. All of the principal sum.

    g. All of the principal sum. (The benefit for any one accident never exceeds the principal sum, even if there are more than two losses.)

69. Only for accidents.

70. a. No.

    b. No.

    c. Yes.

    d. No.

    e. No.

    f. Yes.

71. Nonoccupational AD&D policies do not cover accidents resulting from the insured's employment. Twenty-four hour AD&D policies cover accidents occurring at any time, on or off the job.

72. Non-optional.

73. Optional group insurance.

74. It is usually the same as the benefit of the group life insurance.

75. Until retirement.

76. Traveling on company business.

77. Entirely by the employer.

78. a. Provide 24-hour protection for the employee's entire trip, from the time the employee leaves her home or place of business until she returns.

    b. Cover only accidents involving common carriers.

    c. Cover accidents involving any sort of conveyance, including personal or company-owned vehicles.

79. A public conveyance licensed and used for the transportation of passengers.

80. Either.

81. Accidental death or dismemberment while the insured is a passenger on a common carrier such as an airplane.

82. A single trip, usually on a round-trip basis.

83. Travel accident insurance is sold differently.

84. In vending machines in airports, bus terminals, and railroad stations; from representatives of insurers at large airports; at travel agencies; and by credit card companies as an additional benefit.

85. They make this very limited type of coverage available at low cost.

86. Medical expenses resulting from an accidental injury.

87. Accident medical expense covers accidents only, while regular medical expense covers accidents and diseases. Accident medical expense coverage usually supplements regular medical expense insurance.

88. • Expenses must be incurred within a specified time from the date of the accident.

    • There is an overall maximum benefit for any one accident.

    • Some plans have small deductibles.

89. Medicare beneficiaries must pay deductibles and coinsurance, and there is no limit to their out-of-pocket expenses. They must also pay for services that Medicare does not cover. Medicare supplement insurance reimburses for these expenses.

90. Persons age 65 and older who are eligible for Social Security retirement benefits.

91. Do not pay.

92. a. Stella pays an initial deductible only.

    b. Harold pays the initial deductible,

Medicare pays the rest of hospital charges for the first 60 days, and Harold pays a daily copayment for the remaining 10 days.

c. Sarah pays the initial deductible, Medicare pays the rest of hospital charges for the first 60 days, and Sarah pays a daily copayment for the next 30 days. After 90 days, the same copayment arrangement continues, but Sarah is using up her lifetime supply of 60 extra days. After 150 days, the extra 60 days are gone, and Sarah must pay for all hospital expenses.

d. On the 90ᵗʰ day.

93. Can use some during one hospital stay and some during other stays.

94. Medicare Part A pays all costs of the first 20 days, Edward pays a daily copayment for days 21 through 100, and after the 100ᵗʰ day Edward pays all costs.

95. The same.

96. Only after at least three days in a hospital.

97. a. Up to 21 days (intermittent or consecutive) per spell of illness.

b. Lifetime limit of 210 days.

c. All the blood the beneficiary needs after a deductible of the first three pints.

98. Voluntary.

99. 25 percent.

100. Prescription drugs.

101. Are not. The beneficiary must pay a deductible, 20 percent coinsurance, and all expenses not covered by either Part A or Part B.

102. Must offer Plan A and can offer any other plan.

103. Plan F.

Answers to Practice Exam Questions

1. a

2. a

3. c

4. c

5 DISABILITY INCOME COVERAGE AND LONG-TERM CARE COVERAGE

Disability Income Insurance (Pages 43–48)

1. What is the purpose of disability income insurance?

2. **"Disability income insurance," "income protection insurance,"** and **"loss of time insurance"** are (the same / different).

3. Disability income insurance is offered on (an individual basis / a group basis / both an individual and a group basis).

4. **Long-term disability (LTD) insurance** is the same as (long-term care insurance / group disability income insurance).

5. Disability income policies cover disability caused by (injury only / injury and illness / either).

6. What are the three provisions of a disability income policy that together determine what benefits are payable?

7. What is a **monthly or weekly indemnity**?

8. The monthly or weekly indemnity amount is (determined by the insured's actual loss of income / agreed to in advance by the insurer and the insured).

9. Why would the insured want the monthly indemnity amount to be fairly high?

10. Why would the insured want the monthly indemnity amount to be not too high?

11. Why would the insurer want the monthly indemnity amount to be fairly high?

12. Why would the insurer want the monthly indemnity amount to be not too high?

13. What indemnity amount, in terms of the insured's normal income, would be too high from the point of view of the insurer?

14. Some insurers set maximum indemnity amounts that are a percentage of the insured's income. This percentage is (lower / higher) for high incomes and (lower / higher) for low incomes.

15. Most insurers have a maximum indemnity amount regardless of income. This maximum varies primarily according to what?

16. Why are some insurers reluctant to sell disability income coverage to persons with incomes below a certain level?

17. What is an **elimination period** for disability income insurance?

18. What is the purpose of elimination periods?

♦ 19. The **benefit waiting period** and the elimination period are (the same / different).

♦ 20. What is the **maximum benefit period** in disability income insurance?

♦ 21. The **indemnity limit** and the maximum benefit period are (the same / different).

22. Disability income policies generally pay for a disability (due to any cause / due to a cause covered by the policy only).

♦ 23. What is **total disability**?

♦ 24. What is **residual disability**?

♦ 25. What is **permanent partial disability**?

♦ 26. What is the **own-occupation** definition of total disability?

♦ 27. What is the **any-occupation** definition of total disability?

28. Some policies take a two-period approach to defining total disability. How does this work?

29. A group disability income policy usually uses (the own-occupation definition only / the any-occupation definition only / a two-period approach / either definition but not both).

30. Individual disability income policies use (the own-occupation definition only / the any-occupation definition only / a two-period approach / all of these).

31. An individual disability income policy that uses only (the own-occupation definition / the any-occupation definition) is generally more expensive.

32. What is the purpose of the initial period of own-occupation definition in a two-period approach?

33. What are the advantages of a two-period approach?

34. Karl has a continuing disability. He is able to work, but not in his regular occupation, so he earns 10 percent less than he did before. Under most policies he would be (eligible / not eligible) for residual disability benefits.

35. How is the amount of benefits for residual disability determined?

36. Why do residual disability benefits not compensate for all income loss?

♦ 37. What is **earned income** for the purposes of disability income insurance?

38. Insurers normally base pre-disability income on (the insured's monthly income in the last worked month / average income during a 12- or 24-month period before the disability occurred).

♦ 39. Additional disability income coverages include: **short-term monthly indemnity, social insurance substitute (SIS), future increase option (guaranteed insurability option), return-of-premium option,** and **cost-of-living adjustment (COLA).** Which of these coverages does each of these people have?

a. Janice has the option of responding to inflation by increasing the monthly indemnity amount of her policy at specified future option dates.

b. Susan's policy has a provision that increases benefit payments to compensate for the effects of inflation during a lengthy period of disability.

c. Ted pays an extra premium and in return will get back a percentage of the premiums he has paid if he has not become disabled within a certain period of time.

d. Jane has a coverage that pays her a certain amount every month in addition to the regular monthly payments during the first few months of total disability. This provides additional income until Jane becomes eligible for Social Security disability benefits.

e. Andrew has a coverage that provides additional monthly disability benefits during periods when he is not receiving benefits from government programs.

40. Why is the future increase option also called the guaranteed insurability option?

41. Under the future increase option, how are increases in the monthly indemnity amount limited?

♦ 42. What do **overhead expense insurance** and **key-employee disability income insurance** have in common?

♦ 43. How do **overhead expense insurance** and **key-employee disability income insurance** differ?

44. Which of these expenses are usually covered by overhead expense insurance and which are not?

a. Rent.

b. Utilities.

c. Interest on mortgage payments.

d. Payment on the principal of any indebtedness.

e. The insured's salary.

f. The salaries of other employees.

g. Compensation of any person hired to perform the insured's duties.

h. Purchase of goods and merchandise.

i. Any expenses not regularly and customarily incurred before the disability.

♦ 45. What is the purpose of **disability buyout insurance (business interest insurance)**?

46. How does disability buyout insurance work?

♦ 47. What is **morbidity**?

48. Why has disability income insurance become less profitable and less affordable?

Long-Term Care Insurance (Pages 48–52)

49. What is the purpose of long-term care insurance?

50. Long-term care insurance covers nursing care provided (in a nursing home only / in a nursing home or in the insured's home).

◆ 51. What is meant by **loss of functional capacity**?

◆ 52. What are the six **activities of daily living (ADLs)**?

53. What is transferring?

54. What are the causes of loss of functional capacity?

◆ 55. How does the **elimination period** work in long-term care insurance?

56. (All / Some) long-term care policies have an elimination period.

57. Prior hospitalization or nursing home confinement (is / is not) required for the insured to begin receiving benefits.

◆ 58. What is meant by **benefit period** in long-term care?

59. When does the benefit period begin?

60. When does the benefit period end?

61. Long-term care policies provide that the elimination period must be satisfied (generally only once per lifetime / generally once per benefit period / either, depending on the policy).

62. When an insured is receiving long-term care benefit payments, he (is / is not) required to pay premiums.

63. To be reimbursed by long-term care insurance, home health care services (must be / need not be) provided in the insured's own home.

64. In each of the following cases, will the individual probably receive long-term care benefits or not?

    a. Two years after becoming covered by a long-term care policy, Deborah loses functional capacity as a result of a condition that existed before she became insured.

    b. Robert loses functional capacity due to Alzheimer's disease.

    c. Peter loses functional capacity due to alcoholism.

    d. Sally loses functional capacity due to a self-inflicted injury.

65. What are four types of expenses that most long-term care policies do not pay?

66. Bill has long-term care insurance through an employer-sponsored plan, but is about to retire. Will he lose his coverage?

67. What are the two approaches to dealing with inflation in long-term care insurance?

68. Long-term care insurance has experienced (growth / decline) in recent years.

69. What is the main reason that long-term care insurance is likely to experience growth in the future?

Practice Exam Questions

1. In disability income insurance, the most appropriate monthly indemnity amount is _____ the insured's earned income.

   a. almost the same as

   b. somewhat less than

   c. somewhat more than

   d. the same as

2. Key-employee disability income insurance

   a. pays a preset monthly amount to the business.

   b. pays a preset monthly amount to the employee.

   c. reimburses the business for actual expenses.

   d. reimburses the employee for actual expenses.

3. Long-term care insurance usually pays for care provided in a

   a. drug rehabilitation center.

   b. facility outside the United States.

   c. hospital.

   d. private home.

4. Long-term care insurance usually excludes care needed because of

   a. cognitive impairment.

   b. mental illness.

   c. physical illness.

   d. physical injury.

Answers

1. It protects the insured against loss of income in the event he is unable to work due to an illness or injury.

2. The same.

3. Both an individual and group basis.

4. Group disability income insurance.

5. Either.

6. Monthly or weekly indemnity, elimination period, and maximum benefit period.

7. The amount paid to the insured on a monthly or weekly basis during total disability.

8. Agreed to in advance by the insurer and the insured.

9. To provide her with enough income to live on.

10. The higher the indemnity, the higher the premiums she will pay.

11. The higher the indemnity, the more it earns in premiums.

12. If the amount is too high the insured has a financial incentive to become or remain disabled.

13. Greater than or nearly equal to the insured's normal income.

14. It is lower for high incomes and higher for low incomes.

15. The occupation of the insured.

16. People with limited incomes find it difficult to pay premiums and often let their policies lapse.

17. The period of time at the beginning of a period of disability for which no benefits are payable.

18. They help reduce the insurer's administrative costs and keep premiums affordable by eliminating many small claims.

19. The same.

20. The maximum length of time for which benefits are payable during any one period of disability.

21. The same.

22. Due to a cause covered by the policy only.

23. The complete loss of the ability to earn a living.

24. Reduced earning ability. (The insured is able to work but unable to perform some normal job duties or unable to work full time).

25. Reduced earning ability (same as residual disability).

26. The insured is considered totally disabled if she is unable to engage in her own normal occupation.

27. The insured is considered totally disabled only if she is unable to engage in any gainful occupation for which she is reasonably suited by education, training, or experience.

28. During an initial period of disability, such as the first two or three years, the own-occupation definition applies. After the initial period the any-occupation definition applies.

29. A two-period approach.

30. All of these.

31. The own-occupation definition.

32. It provides an adjustment period during which an insured who will not be able to continue in her previous occupation can get additional training or education.

33. It is less expensive than a strict own-occupation policy, but it provides a period of adjustment during which the own-occupation definition applies.

34. Not eligible. The insured must usually earn an income that is at least 20 percent (25 percent in some policies) less than prior monthly earned income.

35. The insured's earned income during residual disability is compared to his earned income before the disability. The amount of benefits will be a portion of income reduction.

36. Benefits must not make the insured's disabled income exceed or nearly equal her normal income, as this would give her an incentive to remain on disability.

37. Pre-tax income received from salary, wages, fees, commissions, or other remuneration earned by the insured for services performed.

38. Average income during a 12- or 24-month period before the disability occurred.

39. a. Future increase option (guaranteed insurability option).

    b. Cost-of-living adjustment (COLA).

    c. Return-of-premium option.

    d. Short-term monthly indemnity.

    e. Social insurance substitute (SIS).

40. Because the insured has the right to increase the indemnity amount regardless of medical insurability.

41. Increases are both limited to certain stipulated amounts and based on the income growth of the insured.

42. They both protect a business from the loss of earnings that can occur when an important employee is disabled. Also, for both coverages, benefits are paid to the business, not the disabled employee.

43. Overhead expense insurance reimburses for actual expenses; key-employee disability income insurance pays a preset monthly amount.

44. a. Yes.

    b. Yes

    c. Yes.

    d. No.

    e. No.

    f. Yes.

    g. No.

    h. No.

    i. No.

45. It provides the funds for the purchase of the business interest of a partner or stockholder who becomes disabled.

46. The partners or stockholders prepare a formal buy/sell agreement in advance. This agreement provides that if one of them becomes disabled for a certain length of time, generally two years, the disabled person is obliged to sell his interest and the other partners or stockholders are obliged to buy it. The agreement specifies the price (or a formula calculating the price) at which the business interest will be sold.

47. The frequency and severity of illnesses and accidents.

48. Morbidity has increased, claims have increased, and premium rates have gone up.

49. It provides benefits when an insured suffers a loss of functional capacity and so needs the assistance of another person to perform the necessary activities of life.

50. In a nursing home or in the insured's home.

51. The need for assistance to perform some or all of the activities of daily living (ADLs).

52. Bathing, dressing, transferring, toileting, eating, and continence.

53. Moving between the bed and a chair or a wheelchair.

54. The causes may be physical or cognitive, they may result from an injury or a disease (including an organic brain disease), or the cause may simply be aging.

55. Benefits are payable only after a certain number of consecutive days during which the insured suffers loss of functional capacity.

56. Some.

57. Is not.

58. The period during which the insured is receiving benefits.

59. On the first day following the end of the elimination period.

60. After the insured regains functional capacity for an extended period (often 60 days).

61. Either, depending on the policy.

62. Is not.

63. Need not be.

64. a. Probably yes. Benefits are usually provided for preexisting conditions if the loss of capacity occurs more than six (sometimes 12) months after the effective date of the policy.

    b. Probably yes. Although mental, nervous, or emotional disorders are usually excluded, organic brain diseases such as Alzheimer's disease are usually covered.

    c. Probably not. Loss of functional capacity due to alcoholism and drug addiction is usually excluded.

    d. Probably not. Loss of functional capacity due to self-inflicted injuries or attempted suicide is usually excluded.

65. • Expenses incurred any day the insured is confined in a hospital;

• nursing care or home health care expenses covered under other types of health insurance;

• expenses for which reimbursement is available under a government program; or

• expenses for care received outside the United States.

66. Probably not. Generally employees may continue coverage for themselves, spouses, and others by paying premiums directly to the insurer.

67. • The insured is allowed to periodically increase benefits (with an increase in premium).

• An annual increase in benefits is guaranteed. The premium is higher than in the first approach, but it does not increase with the annual benefit increase.

68. Growth.

69. As advances in medical science help us live longer, the likelihood increases that each of us will at some point need long-term care coverage.

Answers to Practice Exam Questions

1. b

2. a

3. d

4. b

6 FLEXIBLE BENEFIT PLANS

Introduction (Page 53)

1. What is a **flexible benefit plan**?

2. What is another name for flexible benefit plans?

3. How does the credit approach to flexible benefits work?

Advantages of Flexible Benefit Plans (Pages 53–54)

4. How does a flexible benefit plan increase employee satisfaction?

5. How does a flexible benefit plan help employers limit health insurance cost increases?

6. How does a flexible benefit plan encourage the use of managed care?

Designing a Flexible Benefit Plan (Pages 54–56)

7. The three basic flexible benefit plan designs are **modular, core-plus,** and **full flexible.** Which of the three designs does each of these describe?

   a. The employer provides multiple options for each type of coverage. Employees freely choose and combine coverages to create a customized benefit package for themselves.

   b. The employer provides three or four benefit packages. Each is designed to meet the needs of a certain broad type of employee, and employees choose among them.

   c. The employer provides a basic package of benefits for all employees as well as additional coverages that employees may choose.

Issues Related to Flexible Benefit Plans (Pages 56–57)

8. Why is planning more difficult under a flexible benefit plan than in the traditional system?

9. How do some employers deal with the unpredictability of flexible benefit plans?

10. H&M Manufacturing has a modular flexible benefit plan with three options. Option A has greater benefits than Options B and C, but premiums are also higher. What will likely happen?

11. What is the phenomenon described in the previous question called?

Practice Exam Questions

1. PIM Corporation grants each of its employees a certain amount of money that she can apply to various health insurance options. This is an example of the _____ approach to flexible benefit plans.

   a. credit

   b. core-plus

   c. full-flexible

   d. modular

2. A disadvantage of flexible benefit plans is

   a. decreased employee satisfaction.

   b. higher health insurance costs.

   c. increased difficulty in planning.

   d. less employee choice.

Answers

1. An arrangement whereby an employer offers its employees a selection of insurance options.

2. Cafeteria plans.

3. The employer provides each employee with an amount of credits that she can apply to whatever combination of benefits she chooses.

4. It allows each employee to make the most of employer benefit dollars and get the benefits he values most.

5. By encouraging employees to use managed care plans.

6. By giving employees financial incentives to choose it.

7. a. Full-flexible.

   b. Modular.

   c. Core-plus.

8. Under a flexible benefit plan, it may be hard to predict how many employees will choose which options.

9. They begin with a plan design that offers relatively few options and then gradually introduce more choices.

10. Those who have more health problems will choose Option A, so that Option A will have a disproportionate number of the people who will actually incur expenses.

11. Adverse selection (also known as anti-selection or selection against the insurer).

Answers to Practice Exam Questions

1. a

2. c

7 THE INSURANCE CONTRACT

Introduction (Page 59)

◆ 1. What is a **contract**?

2. Who are the parties to an insurance contract?

3. What is the basic agreement of an insurance contract?

4. In addition to the basic agreement, what is set forth in an insurance contract?

5. The parties to an insurance contract (may make any agreement they wish / are limited in the agreement they may make by laws and regulations).

The Basic Elements of a Contract (Pages 59–61)

6. What four elements must all contracts have to be legally binding?

◆ 7. What is **consideration**?

8. In an insurance contract, what is the consideration made by the prospective policyholder?

9. What is the consideration made by the insurer?

10. For a contract to be valid, consideration must be made by (one party / both parties / one or both parties).

◆ 11. What occurs when there is a **meeting of the minds**?

◆ 12. What does it mean to say that a party is acting in **good faith**?

13. Why is good faith on the part of both parties necessary for a meeting of the minds?

◆ 14. What does it mean to **rescind** a contract?

15. Even if there is good faith on the part of both parties, there may not be a meeting of the minds. How can this happen?

16. If it is discovered that there was no meeting of the minds, the contract (must be / may be) rescinded.

◆ 17. What is **capacity to contract**?

18. Why is capacity to contract necessary for meeting of the minds?

19. What classes of persons are not assumed to have capacity to contract?

◆ 20. What does **offer and acceptance** mean?

21. An agent representing HHH Insurance Company contacts Jonathan and tries to sell him a major medical insurance policy. Is the agent making an offer?

22. Jonathan submits an application for the policy and pays the first premium. Is Jonathan making an offer?

23. HHH Insurance Company rejects Jonathan's application but makes a counteroffer of a modified policy with a higher rate. Is the contract now formed?

The Contract, the Policy, and the Application (Pages 61–62)

24. An insurance contract normally consists of what two documents?

25. A contract may exist even if no policy has been issued. How?

26. There may be no legally binding contract even if a policy has been issued. How?

27. What information does an insurance policy contain?

28. What information does an insurance application contain?

◆ 29. What is a **representation**?

30. What responsibilities does the applicant have concerning representations?

31. What responsibilities does the insurer have concerning representations made by the applicant?

Legal Principles of Health Insurance Contracts (Pages 62–63)

◆ 32. What kind of contract does each of the following sentences describe? (The kinds of contracts described include: **unilateral contract, conditional contract, aleatory contract,** and **contract of adhesion.**)

   a. Offered on a take-it-or-leave-it basis by a party of superior strength and knowledge to a party of limited resources and little expertise.

   b. One of the parties may recover a great deal more in value than she has parted with, depending upon the occurrence of some future contingent event.

   c. A party to this contract must perform only on the condition that a given event occurs.

   d. Only one of the parties makes a promise.

33. Why are health insurance contracts unilateral?

34. Claudia has entered into an insurance contract as a policyholder. She stops paying premiums. The insurer (can / cannot) sue her for failure to perform under the contract.

35. Why are health insurance contracts conditional?

36. Why are health insurance contracts aleatory?

37. Why are insurance contracts contracts of adhesion?

38. How does the fact that insurance contracts are contracts of adhesion affect their interpretation by courts?

✦ 39. What is the **doctrine of reasonable expectations?**

40. What is the purpose of the readability standards that most states require for insurance policies?

Definitions in the Insurance Contract (Pages 63–64)

41. Why are definitions of the key words and phrases in a contract necessary for a meeting of the minds?

42. Different insurers generally use (similar definitions / different definitions / both).

43. Why do definitions change over time?

Contract Execution (Pages 64–65)

44. Normally, an applicant must sign the application in the presence of (a notary / an insurance agent / an employee of the insurer).

45. If an agent is involved, why does he sign the application?

46. (The insurer / The agent) ensures that all legal requirements are met.

47. To signify that the insurer is offering coverage, the policy is signed by (an agent representing the insurer / an authorized executive officer of the insurer).

48. Why does the agent countersign the policy before it is submitted to the applicant?

49. At what point does the insurer make a legally binding offer?

Contract Renewal and Revision (Page 65)

✦ 50. What is the **term** of an insurance policy?

✦ 51. What is **renewal**?

52. Which kinds of health insurance policies are not usually renewable?

✦ 53. What is **contract revision**?

54. An insurance contract can be revised by (the insurer only / the policyholder only/ either party / both parties in agreement only).

✦ 55. What is a **rider**?

✦ 56. What is an **endorsement** or **amendment**?

Emerging Trends (Page 65)

57. Ensuring that contracts are in compliance with state insurance laws has become more difficult. Why?

Practice Exam Questions

1. In an insurance contract, the consideration made by the applicant is the
   I. application.
   II. first premium.
   III. promise to continue paying premiums.

   a. I and II only.

   b. I and III only.

   c. II and III only.

   d. I, II, and III.

2. One of the parties to a contract unintentionally fails to provide important information to the other party. What necessary element of a contract is missing in this situation?

   a. Capacity to contract.

   b. Consideration.

   c. Good faith.

   d. Meeting of the minds.

3. In determining if an application for insurance constitutes an offer in the legal sense, the key question is:

   a. Does the applicant have the same understanding of the agreement as the insurer?

   b. Has the applicant provided all relevant information accurately and completely?

   c. Has the applicant taken all necessary steps so that if the insurer accepts the application a contract is formed?

   d. Is the applicant of legal age and mentally competent?

4. In a unilateral contract, one party

   a. has superior strength and knowledge.

   b. makes a consideration and the other does not.

   c. makes a promise and the other does not.

   d. makes an offer and the other accepts.

Answers

1. A voluntary, written, legally binding agreement between two parties.

2. The insurer and the policyholder.

3. The insurer agrees to compensate the policyholder for a loss in return for the premiums paid to the insurer.

4. The terms and conditions of the agreement and the rights and obligations of the parties.

5. Are limited in the agreement they may make by laws and regulations.

6. Consideration, meeting of the minds, capacity to contract, and offer and acceptance.

7. What each party to a contract does or gives in exchange for what the other party does or gives.

8. The submission of the application for insurance and the payment of the premium.

9. Its promise to pay the benefits described in the policy.

10. Both parties.

11. Both parties have the same understanding of the agreement and of their respective obligations and rights under the contract.

12. The party does not have the intention of deceiving or taking unfair advantage of the other party.

13. Without good faith, the parties do not truly have the same understanding of the agreement and so a meeting of the minds has not been reached.

14. To cancel it.

15. A meeting of minds may not occur because, due to an honest mistake, important information is missing or incorrect, so that one of the parties does not have an accurate understanding of the terms of the agreement.

16. May be. (The parties may agree to modify the contract.)

17. The ability to understand the terms of a contract.

18. Meeting of the minds depends on an accurate understanding of the contract by both parties.

19. Minors and those determined by a court to be mentally incompetent.

20. One party makes an offer and the other party accepts it.

21. No, he is only proposing a product to a customer. He is not making a legal offer because he has not taken all necessary action so that if Jonathan takes action the contract is formed. In other words, the agent's action is not potentially the next to last step in the process.

22. Yes, Jonathan has taken all necessary action so that if the insurer takes action (approving the application, accepting payment, and issuing the requested policy) the contract is formed.

23. No. An offer has been made but acceptance has not occurred. If Jonathan accepts HHH's counteroffer, the contract is formed.

24. The policy and the application submitted by the policyholder.

25. The actions of the parties and the documents involved may otherwise satisfy the legal requirements for the existence of a contract.

26. If either party fails to meet any of the essential elements for the formation of a contract, no contract exists.

27. The terms of the coverage that the insurer will provide.

28. Information about the prospective policyholder.

29. A statement that supplies information or facts that the other party to the contract believes to be true.

30. The representations she makes must be true—that is, the information must be accurate and complete.

31. If an answer on the application is clearly ambiguous or incomplete, it is the insurer's responsibility to obtain clarification before it issues the policy.

32. a. Contract of adhesion.

    b. Aleatory contract.

    c. Conditional contract.

    d. Unilateral contract.

33. Because the insurer promises to reimburse the insured for stipulated losses, but the

policyholder makes no promise to do or to pay anything.

34. Cannot. A policyholder must pay premiums if she wants the policy to continue, but she has not promised to do so.

35. Because the insurer must perform (pay the benefits) only if an event (a covered loss) occurs.

36. The insured may receive a very large amount in benefits after the payment of only one premium.

37. The insurer has superior strength and knowledge compared to the policyholder.

38. Because the two parties are considered not to have equal bargaining power, when there is a dispute over the meaning of a contract, the courts generally interpret the contract in a manner that is most favorable to the policyholder.

39. If circumstances suggest that the policyholder expected something different from what the written contract states, and if the court considers the policyholder's expectations more reasonable than the conclusion arrived at by strict adherence to the contract language, the court must find in favor of the policyholder.

40. To ensure that the language and format of policies are understandable to the average consumer.

41. Meeting of the minds means that both parties have the same understanding of the agreement. Without definitions, each party might have a different understanding of terms.

42. Both. (Some terms are usually defined differently, others vary little from policy to policy.)

43. Because of legislation, court decisions, and insurance industry efforts to provide more liberal coverage.

44. An insurance agent.

45. To attest that the applicant signed the application in his presence and to fulfill regulatory requirements.

46. The insurer.

47. An authorized executive officer of the insurer.

48. To fulfill legal requirements, to prove the identity of the agent and make his participation a matter of record, and to ensure that insurance sales will be conducted only by agents licensed to do so in the state.

49. When it submits the signed policy to the applicant.

50. The period stipulated by the contract during which the contract will be in force.

51. The continuation of the policy at the end of the original term.

52. Certain accident policies and other health insurance coverage designed to cover short-term risk situations. These policies are issued for a single term and must terminate at the end of that term.

53. The modification of the provisions of a contract.

54. Both parties in agreement.

55. A document added to a contract to modify or amend the contract.

56. A rider.

57. Mergers, acquisitions, joint ventures, and the development of subsidiary companies has meant that many companies are now operating in many different states, each with its own insurance laws.

Answers to Practice Exam Questions

1. a

2. d

3. c

4. c

8 PROVISIONS OF MEDICAL EXPENSE INSURANCE CONTRACTS

The Definition of a Dependent (Pages 67–68)

1. The definition of "dependent" varies (greatly / little) from policy to policy.

2. What is the typical definition of a policyholder's or employee's spouse?

3. A spouse (is / is not) considered a dependent in cases of legal separation.

4. Tom and Wilma have a large family. Which of their children would probably be considered dependents under Wilma's medical expense insurance?

   a. Timmy is 12. He lives with Tom's former wife and is principally supported by her.

   b. Bruce is 14. He lives with Tom and Wilma and is supported by them.

   c. Scott is 17. He is married and largely self-supporting.

   d. Bill is 22. He is a full-time student and financially dependent on Tom and Wilma.

   e. Betty is 29 and has been mentally retarded all of her life. She works but is not capable of earning enough to live on.

   f. Will is 27 and became physically handicapped due to an accident last year. He also works but is not capable of earning enough to live on.

5. Dependent children may include (biological children and stepchildren / biological children only).

General Provisions (Pages 68–69)

◆ 6. What does the **entire contract clause** state?

7. (All / Some) contracts have an entire contract clause.

8. In a health insurance contract, what documents generally make up the entire contract?

9. Typically, an insurance contract gives the authority to act on behalf of the insurance company in any modification of the contract to (agents and brokers / officers of the company).

◆ 10. What does the **consideration clause** of an insurance contract state?

Provisions Related to Premiums (Pages 69–70)

11. Most group policyholders pay premiums (monthly / annually / semi-annually / quarterly).

12. Most policies guarantee initial premium rates for (six months / 12 months / two years).

13. After the period of initial guaranteed rates, rates may usually be changed (at any time / on anniversary dates of the policy / on any premium due date).

14. Generally, if the terms of a policy are changed, premium rates can be changed (at any time that terms change / at any time except during a period of guaranteed initial rates / only on a premium due date).

15. If premium rates are changed at renewal, the insurer (must modify the policy document / can simply notify the policyholder in writing).

16. If a policyholder stops paying premiums, the insurer can (sue the policyholder for breach of contract / terminate the contract and stop coverage / either).

17. What is a **grace period** in the context of an insurance contract?

18. The grace period is typically (10 days / 31 days / 60 days).

19. Nikki pays a premium on her policy after the due date but before the end of the grace period. Her coverage (will / will not) be cancelled. She (will / will not) have to pay an interest penalty on the late payment.

20. If a group policyholder does not pay a premium by the end of the grace period and the insurer terminates the contract, the policyholder still has the obligation to pay the premium for the grace period. Why?

Provisions Related to Benefits and Claims (Pages 70–71)

21. What does the **insuring clause** of an insurance contract do?

22. What does the insuring clause say about claims?

23. What do the **benefit provisions** of an insurance contract do?

24. The insurance laws of some states require that a contract set three time limits related to claims. What are these time limits for?

25. Usually, the time limit for submitting a claim to an insurance company is (20 / 60 / 90) days from the date of loss.

26. Usually, the time limit for submitting proofs of loss is (20 / 60 / 90) days from the date of loss.

27. Usually, the time limit for the insurance company to make payment is (20 / 60 / 90) days after proof of loss has been filed.

✦ 28. What is **overinsurance**?

29. Why does overinsurance occur?

30. How can overinsurance lead to higher premiums?

✦ 31. What does a **coordination of benefits (COB)** provision do?

32. The COB provisions of most group policies usually coordinate with (other group policies only / individual policies only / both).

✦ 33. What is **assignment of benefits**?

34. Most health insurance contracts (allow / do not allow) the policyholder to make an assignment of benefits.

35. If an insurance contract does not require an insurer to allow assignment of benefits, the insurer will (rarely / often) allow it.

✦ 36. What are **unassigned benefits**?

37. Unassigned benefits (revert to the insurer / are paid to a person stipulated in the contract).

Provisions Related to the Beginning and End of Coverage (Page 72)

✦ 38. What is the **effective date** of a policy?

39. An insurer can terminate a contract (on any premium due date / on the first policy anniversary only / on any policy anniversary / on any premium due date on or after the first policy anniversary).

40. Which of these must give advance notice before terminating a contract? (An insurer / a group policyholder / an individual policyholder).

41. The normal amount of time for advance notice of termination is (31 / 60 / 90) days.

42. How does an individual policyholder terminate an insurance contract?

Practice Exam Questions

1. Under most medical expense insurance policies, which of the following would be considered a dependent of an insured?

   a. A legally separated but not divorced spouse.

   b. A 23-year-old child who is a college student supported by the insured.

   c. A 25-year-old child who became handicapped after becoming an adult.

   d. An 18-year-old child who is self-supporting.

2. The clause of a health insurance contract that allows the insured to request the payment of benefits directly to her doctor is the _____ clause.

   a. assignment of benefits

   b. ceding of payments

   c. coordination of benefits

   d. facility of payments

3. The clause that states that the insurer is issuing the policy in exchange for the application and the payment of the first premium is the _____ clause.

   a. assignment of benefits

   b. consideration

   c. entire contract

   d. insuring

4. The term "unassigned benefits" usually refers to benefits due to an insured who

   a. has not assigned them to a health care provider.

   b. has not filed a claim for them.

   c. is no longer covered by the policy.

   d. is no longer living.

Answers

1. Little.

2. The person to whom the policyholder or employee is legally married.

3. Is not.

4. a. No.

   b. Yes.

   c. No.

   d. Yes.

   e. Yes.

   f. No.

5. Biological children and stepchildren.

6. What documents make up the contract.

7. All.

8. The policy and the application of the policyholder (and sometimes applications of the insureds for group policies).

9. Officers of the company.

10. That the insurer is issuing the policy (its consideration) in exchange for the application and the payment of the first premium (the policyholder's consideration).

11. Monthly.

12. 12 months.

13. On any premium due date.

14. At any time that terms change.

15. Can simply notify the policyholder in writing.

16. Terminate the contract and stop coverage only.

17. A period after the premium due date during which the insured's coverage remains in force even if the premium has not been paid.

18. 31 days.

19. Her coverage will not be cancelled, and she will not have to pay an interest penalty.

20. Because coverage was in force and the insurer was liable for claims.

21. It expresses in general terms the insurer's promise to pay benefits.

22. It specifies that proof of loss must be submitted to the insurer before claim payment will be made.

23. They state under what conditions the insurer will have the obligation to pay benefits, how the payment will be made, and what the benefits will be. They also state any limitations or exclusions.

24. For submitting a claim to the insurance company, for submitting proofs of loss, and for the insurance company to make payment.

25. 20 days.

26. 90 days.

27. 60 days.

28. Overinsurance occurs when a medical expense of an individual is covered by more than one health insurance policy.

29. In many families both husband and wife have employer-sponsored group policies, and their dependent children are covered by both policies. Also, some people have one or more individual policies, often in addition to group policies.

30. If claims are filed with two insurers for the same expense, the insured may receive more in benefits than he actually spent on expenses. This gives the insured an incentive to use more services than he really needs, which increases costs to the insurer, making it necessary for the insurer to raise premiums.

31. It allows the insurer to take into account the total benefits paid to a person who has overlapping coverage under more than one policy and ensures that the total benefit payments he receives never exceed his total expenses.

32. Other group policies only.

33. An insurance contract usually stipulates that the insurer pays all benefits directly to the insured, who must then pay the provider of services (such as a doctor). The insured may request that benefits be assigned (paid directly) to the provider.

34. Allow.

35. Often.

36. Benefits that remain unpaid when the insured dies.

37. Are paid to a person stipulated in the contract.

38. The date on which the insured begins to be covered by the policy.

39. On any premium due date on or after the first policy anniversary.

40. Insurers and group policyholders.

41. 31 days.

42. Simply by stopping payment of premiums.

Answers to Practice Exam Questions

1. b

2. a

3. b

4. d

9 PROVISIONS OF GROUP MEDICAL EXPENSE INSURANCE CONTRACTS

Introduction (Page 73)

1. The group covered by group health insurance is most often made up of the (members of a union / members of an association / employees of a business).

2. In employer-sponsored group health insurance, the policyholder is (the employer / the employee / both).

3. In employer-sponsored group health insurance, the insured is (the employer / the employee / both).

4. In employer-sponsored group health insurance, who pays the premiums? (The employer / the employee / either or both).

One Policy or Multiple Policies? (Pages 73–74)

◆ 5. What are **lines of coverage**?

6. What are the major lines of coverage?

7. When an employer provides different lines of coverage to its employees, which of these approaches can be taken? (All lines of coverage are combined in one policy / there is a separate policy for each major line of coverage / some lines are combined and others are not / all of these).

8. What is the advantage of combining all lines of coverage into one policy?

The Group Application (Page 74)

9. What information is included in the long form of the application for group insurance but not in the short form?

10. If the short form is used, how is underwriting information obtained?

Enrollment of Insureds (Pages 74–75)

◆ 11. What does it mean to **enroll** an employee in a group health insurance plan?

12. Why must employees be enrolled in a group health plan?

13. How do employees usually enroll?

14. If employees pay a portion of the premium, what must they authorize in their enrollment cards?

15. Minimum enrollment requirements may be expressed as (a percentage of all employees eligible to participate in the plan / a numerical minimum / either or both).

16. What is the most common reason for an insurer's termination of a group policy?

Beginning of Coverage (Pages 75–76)

✦ 17. What is the **effective date** of a group health insurance policy?

18. The effective date of a group contract is established by (the insurer / the policyholder / both).

19. When an insurer takes over the coverage of a group from another insurer, what arrangement is made so that continuous coverage is provided to the insureds?

20. Michelle is hired by Markon Corporation. Markon provides a group health insurance plan to its employees. However, Michelle is not covered by this plan right away. What is the most likely reason for this?

21. Michelle probably will have to wait to receive coverage for (one to three months / six to nine months / nine to 12 months).

22. What is the likely reason that Markon's plan has a probationary waiting period?

✦ 23. What is an **eligibility date**?

24. If an individual joins a covered group, when is her eligibility date (normally)?

25. If an employee joins a covered group and coverage is automatically extended to all employees, when does her coverage begin?

26. If an employee joins a covered group and coverage is optional, when does her coverage begin?

27. Assuming Markon's plan is typical, if Michelle wants to be given group coverage automatically, she should enroll within (31 / 60 / 90) days after her eligibility date.

28. Michelle does not enroll immediately after her eligibility date. Six months later she decides to enroll. What might she have to do?

✦ 29. What is a **late entry**?

✦ 30. What is **evidence of insurability**?

31. What is the purpose of requiring evidence of insurability?

Administrative Responsibilities (Pages 76–77)

32. The work of administering a group health plan is typically done by (employees of the insurer / employees of the policyholder / both).

33. What are some of the administrative tasks that policyholder personnel typically do?

34. Maintaining records on the insured is the responsibility of (the insurer / the policyholder / either).

35. In some cases the policyholder must provide the insurer with information on changes in classification or status of covered individuals. Why?

36. If an error or omission occurs in the record keeping of a group policy, benefits are based on (the correct information / the records).

37. David works at Tresor, Inc. and is covered by Tresor's group health insurance plan. Then David leaves Tresor. However, Tresor mistakenly fails to report to its insurer that David has left. David falls ill. Is he covered by Tresor's group plan?

Experience Refunds (Page 77)

38. BigState Insurance Company provides group health insurance to Arkon Company. BigState charges Arkon a certain level of premiums, based on BigState's prediction of the level of claims Arkon employees will make. However, Arkon employees' claims turn out to be much lower than predicted, and BigState takes in much more in premiums than it pays in claims. Under what circumstances must BigState give Arkon a refund?

39. Whether an experience refund must be paid is based on data as of what date?

40. In what forms may a policyholder receive an experience refund?

Termination and Continuation of Coverage (Pages 77–79)

41. In an employer-sponsored group plan, what are the five circumstances in which an employee's coverage is normally terminated?

42. In a union or association group policy, when does a member's coverage terminate?

43. When does the coverage of an employee's dependent terminate?

♦ 44. What is **COBRA**?

45. Under COBRA, terminated employees have the right to continue group medical insurance coverage for up to (6 / 18 / 36) months.

46. The right to continuation of coverage granted by COBRA applies to employers of (20 / 50 / 100) or more employees.

47. COBRA applies to any terminated employee, except those who (leave without two weeks' notice / are terminated for gross misconduct).

48. COBRA (applies / does not apply) to employees who are not terminated but whose hours are being reduced so that they are no longer eligible for coverage.

49. COBRA (applies / does not apply) to an employee's dependents who lose their eligibility for coverage.

50. Continued coverage under COBRA is paid by the (employee / employer / government).

51. Continued coverage of dependents under COBRA lasts up to (6 / 18 / 36) months.

◆ 52. What is the principal right granted by the federal **Family and Medical Leave Act of 1993?**

53. How much leave can be taken under the Family and Medical Leave Act?

54. For what three reasons can leave can be taken under the Family and Medical Leave Act?

55. How does the Family and Medical Leave Act affect health insurance coverage?

◆ 56. What is a **conversion privilege**?

57. What conditions must the person requesting conversion meet in these areas?

   a. Length of coverage.

   b. Eligibility for coverage.

   c. Application.

   d. Continuation of coverage.

58. A person taking advantage of the privilege of conversion (is / is not) required to give evidence of insurability.

Practice Exam Questions

1. What is the most common reason that an insurer terminates a group policy?

   a. Adverse selection.

   b. Failure to meet or maintain minimum enrollment requirements.

   c. Failure to pay premiums.

   d. Poor administration on the part of the employer.

2. The Consolidated Omnibus Budget Reconciliation Act of 1985 (COBRA) does <u>not</u> grant the right to continuation of coverage to employees who

   a. are fired for gross misconduct.

   b. become ineligible for group health insurance because of a reduction of hours.

   c. leave without giving two weeks' notice.

   d. work for a company with only 50 employees.

3. The group health insurance coverage of all of these people is being terminated. Which one would most likely have the right to convert to individual coverage?

   a. Bill has been insured under the group policy for only six months.

   b. Carol is eligible for another group plan with similar coverage.

   c. Charley fails to apply for individual coverage within 31 days of termination of the group coverage.

   d. John applies for individual coverage but fails to pay the first premium within 31 days of termination of the group coverage.

Answers

1. The employees of a business.

2. The employer.

3. The employee.

4. Either or both.

5. Types of insurance coverage.

6. Life insurance, medical expense insurance, accidental death and dismemberment insurance, dental insurance, disability income insurance, and long-term care insurance.

7. All of these.

8. It avoids duplication of policy provisions that are common to all coverages.

9. Information provided by the employer for underwriting.

10. The agent puts the information on worksheets, which she gives to the insurer.

11. To officially record the employee as being covered.

12. So that there is a clear understanding by the insurer and the employer of which individuals are covered by the policy.

13. By filling out enrollment cards.

14. Payroll deductions.

15. Either or both.

16. The failure to meet or maintain minimum enrollment requirements.

17. The date on which the insureds begin to be covered by the policy.

18. Both.

19. The effective date of the new contract immediately follows the termination date of the old one.

20. Markon probably has a probationary waiting period for individuals joining the group.

21. One to three months.

22. To eliminate the cost of maintaining records for employees who do not stay for very long.

23. The date an employee becomes eligible for coverage.

24. The day after her probationary waiting period ends.

25. On her eligibility date.

26. Any time on or after her eligibility date, as soon as she has filled out an enrollment card and authorized payroll deductions.

27. 31 days.

28. Provide evidence of insurability.

29. An individual who does not join a group plan in the 31 days following his eligibility date and decides to join later.

30. Health and other information proving that the applicant is an acceptable insurance risk.

31. To prevent a person from seeking insurance only after she has contracted an illness.

32. Both.

33. Preparing premium statements, processing enrollments and terminations, issuing

certificates of insurance, certifying eligibility for coverage when there is a claim, and processing claims for medical care benefits in some cases.

34. Either (stipulated by the contract).

35. The changes affect the coverage of the individuals.

36. The correct information.

37. No. Even if a policyholder fails to report to the insurer the termination of an individual's coverage, the coverage does in fact terminate.

38. If there is an experience refund provision in the contract.

39. The policy anniversary date.

40. In cash, applied to subsequent premiums, or left on deposit with the insurer.

41. • The employee ceases to be employed by the policyholder.

   • The employee remains employed by the policyholder, but changes jobs so that she is no longer in a class of employees eligible for coverage under the plan.

   • The employee (or the policyholder) stops paying premiums.

   • The group policy is terminated.

   • The group policy is amended so that the class of employees to which the employee belongs is no longer eligible for coverage.

42. When she ceases to be a member.

43. When the employee's insurance terminates, or when the dependent no longer meets the policy's definition of an eligible dependent (such as when a child becomes an adult or when spouses are legally separated).

44. The federal Consolidated Omnibus Budget Reconciliation Act of 1985.

45. 18 months.

46. 20.

47. Are terminated for gross misconduct.

48. Applies.

49. Applies.

50. Employee.

51. 36 months.

52. The right of eligible employees to take unpaid leave for family or medical reasons.

53. 12 work-weeks of unpaid leave during a 12-month period.

54. • The birth of a child or the arrival of an adopted or foster child;

   • the care of a child, spouse, or parent who has a serious health condition; or

   • a serious health condition of the employee himself that prevents performance of his job.

55. The act requires that any employee who is out on family or medical leave continue to be enrolled in a health insurance plan during that leave.

56. Under a conversion privilege, employees and dependents whose coverage under a group medical expense policy terminates have the right to continue coverage on an individual basis.

57. a. He must have been insured under the group policy for at least three months.

   b. He must not be eligible for similar coverage under another group plan.

   c. He must usually apply in writing and pay the first premium within 31 days of termination of the group coverage.

   d. In some states any applicable continuation of coverage must have expired.

58. Is not.

Answers to Practice Exam Questions

   1. b

   2. a

   3. a

10 PROVISIONS OF INDIVIDUAL MEDICAL EXPENSE INSURANCE CONTRACTS

Introduction (Page 81)

1. In individual insurance, the policyholder is a (business / private person).

2. In individual insurance, the policyholder purchases coverage for (herself only / herself and sometimes her dependents).

The Individual Application (Pages 81–82)

3. What three kinds of information does the applicant supply in an individual medical expense insurance application?

4. What kind of information must the individual applicant supply for underwriting purposes?

5. The answers to questions on an individual application must be (absolutely accurate / accurate to the best of the applicant's knowledge / either, depending on the question).

Schedule of Benefits (Page 82)

6. What is the purpose of a **schedule of benefits**?

7. What is a **policy specifications page**?

Notice of the Right of Examination (Page 82)

8. What is the **right of examination**?

9. Where in an individual policy must a notice of the right of examination appear?

10. Typically, the policyholder has the right of examination for (10 days / 31 days / 3 months).

11. What is another name for the right of examination?

Effective Date (Pages 82–83)

12. Customarily, individual coverage becomes effective after (the first premium is paid / the policy is delivered to the applicant / both).

13. (All / Some / No) policies have a provision stating that coverage will not become effective unless the applicant is in good health at the time of policy delivery.

Renewal Provisions (Pages 83–84)

♦ 14. What does it mean to say that a policy is **renewable**?

15. (All / Most / Some) individual medical expense policies are renewable.

16. Renewable policies fall into four basic categories, according to the rights of the policyholder to renew. What are they?

17. Which category gives the policyholder the most rights?

18. Which category gives the policyholder the least rights?

19. In a noncancellable policy, as long as the policyholder pays the premiums, the insurer cannot do three things. What are they?

20. When do noncancellable policies often become cancellable?

21. The policyholder has the same rights under a guaranteed renewable policy as under a noncancellable policy, with what exception?

22. In a guaranteed renewable policy, an insurer can raise premium rates for (individuals / broad categories of people / both).

23. What are some the circumstances under which an insurer can refuse to renew a policy that is "nonrenewable for stated reasons only"?

24. In an optionally renewable policy, (the policyholder / insurer) has the option of renewing or not.

25. Typically, when can an insurer exercise its option not to renew?

26. If an insurer does not want to continue a policy on the same terms, what can it do instead of flatly refusing to renew the policy?

♦ 27. **Nonrenewal** or **cancellation**? Isis Insurance Company's contract with Jack gives it the option of renewing Jack's policy or not at the end of the term of the policy and thereafter on any premium due date. At the end of the term Isis decides not to continue coverage. This is an example of (nonrenewal / cancellation).

♦ 28. **Nonrenewal** or **cancellation**? Isis has the same policy with Woody, and Isis decides to discontinue coverage before the end of the term. This is an example of (nonrenewal / cancellation).

29. (All / Some / No) states prohibit cancellation.

30. Cancellation is (frequent / rare).

31. Advance notice is required for (cancellation / nonrenewal / both).

32. Under what circumstance may a refund be due to the policyholder after cancellation?

33. HIPAA requires most individual medical expense policies to be (noncancellable / guaranteed renewable / nonrenewable for stated reasons only / optionally renewable).

34. Under what circumstances are insurers allowed to nonrenew policies subject to this requirement of HIPAA?

Model Laws (Pages 84–85)

35. In the United States, the insurance laws and regulations of the various states are (very different / based on model laws and therefore largely uniform / based on model laws and therefore somewhat uniform).

36. Who are the members of the National Association of Insurance Commissioners (NAIC)?

37. The NAIC develops model laws and (mandates / recommends) that states adopt them.

38. If states adopt NAIC model laws, they (must adopt them in their totality / may adopt them only in part or with modifications).

39. In cases where different insurers are governed by the same model laws, (in order to adhere to these laws, their policies must have the same wording and structure / their policies can adhere to these laws even with quite different wording and structure).

40. Match the NAIC model law with the description. The model laws are: the Individual Accident and Sickness Insurance Minimum Standards Act; the Model Life and Health Insurance Policy Language Simplification Act; the Official Guide for Filing and Approval of Accident and Health Contracts; the Uniform Policy Provisions Law (UPPL).

   a. Establishes standards regarding readability.

   b. Specifies mandatory and optional provisions for use in all health insurance policies.

   c. Sets forth standards for policy language, type size, policy provisions, exclusions, and limitations.

   d. Designates several categories for basic forms of coverage with required minimum benefit levels for each.

Provisions Required by the Uniform Policy Provisions Law (UPPL) (Pages 85–86)

♦ 41. What does the **Time Limit On Certain Defenses Provision** of the UPPL state?

42. The Time Limit On Certain Defenses Provision of the UPPL does not apply if the policyholder knowingly made them with the intent to defraud, but this condition is of limited usefulness to insurers. Why?

♦ 43. What does the UPPL's **Incontestable Clause** do?

44. Which of the renewal categories does the Incontestable Clause apply to?

(Noncancellable / guaranteed renewable / nonrenewable for stated reasons only / optionally renewable).

45. How do the Time Limit On Certain Defenses Provision and the Incontestable Clause affect preexisting conditions?

46. What does a reinstatement provision do?

✦ 47. What does the **10-day delay provision** usually state?

48. Under UPPL provisions, the insured must notify the insurer of a loss within (20 / 60 / 90) days after the loss or as soon as is reasonably possible.

49. Under UPPL provisions, the insurer must provide claims forms to the insured within (15 / 60 / 90) days after the insured gives notice of a claim.

50. Under UPPL provisions, the insured must normally submit proof of a loss (15 / 60 / 90) days after the date of the loss.

51. Under UPPL provisions, the insured must wait at least (20 / 60 / 90) days after submitting proof of loss before starting legal action against the insurer.

52. What is the purpose of the waiting period for legal action?

53. Under UPPL provisions, the insured is prohibited from bringing legal action more than (one / three / five) years after the end of the 90-day proof period.

Optional Provisions of Individual Policies (Page 87)

✦ 54. What are **optional provisions**?

55. What are common optional provisions in these areas?

   a. Change of occupation.

   b. Unpaid premiums.

   c. Misstatement of age.

Summary (Page 87)

56. What are three ways in which individual health insurance policies address the fact that individuals who purchase health insurance do not usually have the ability to knowledgeably review all the language of an insurance policy, as does a large business or group?

Practice Exam Questions

1. The "right of examination" gives a prospective policyholder the right to examine an insurance policy and choose not to buy it

   a. before submitting an application for coverage.

   b. after submitting an application but before paying the first premium.

   c. after submitting the application and paying the first premium, but before the insurer accepts the application and issues the policy.

   d. after submitting the application and paying the first premium and after the insurer accepts the application and issues the policy.

2. Under this category of policy, the only change the insurer can make without the consent of the policyholder is in premium rates.

   a. Guaranteed renewable.

   b. Noncancellable.

   c. Nonrenewable for stated reasons only.

   d. Optionally renewable.

3. The cancellation of health insurance policies is

   a. common and legal in all states.

   b. rare but legal in all states.

   c. rare and illegal in some states.

   d. illegal in all states.

4. The Incontestable Clause addresses

   a. the insurer's right to contest a claim.

   b. the policyholder's right to contest a claim decision.

   c. the insurer's right to contest a policy.

   d. the policyholder's right to contest a policy.

Answers

1. Private person.

2. Herself and sometimes her dependents.

3. Information about herself and any other persons proposed for coverage, information about the coverage she desires, and information needed for underwriting.

4. Past medical history of those to be insured, other risk factors, other insurance coverage that the insured may have, and the insured's occupation and earnings.

5. Either, depending on the question.

6. To make benefit provisions clear and easily understandable to the individual policyholder.

7. A schedule of benefits.

8. The right of the policyholder, after he has paid the premium and received the policy, to examine the policy and choose not to buy the coverage.

9. On the front page.

10. 10 days.

11. The 10-day-free-look provision.

12. Both.

13. Some.

14. It can be continued after the initial term.

15. Most.

16. Noncancellable, guaranteed renewable, nonrenewable for stated reasons only, and optionally renewable.

17. Noncancellable.

18. Optionally renewable.

19. It cannot cancel or refuse to renew the policy, make any unilateral changes in any provisions of the policy, or raise the premium rates.

20. When the insured reaches a certain age, usually 50 or older.

21. The insurer may make changes in premium rates.

22. Broad categories of people only.

23. When the policyholder reaches a certain age; when the policyholder ceases to be employed; or when the insurer nonrenews all policies bearing the same form number as the policyholder's policy.

24. The insurer.

25. At the end of the term of the policy, and thereafter on any premium due date.

26. It can set conditions for renewal.

27. Nonrenewal.

28. Cancellation.

29. Some.

30. Rare.

31. Both.

32. If cancellation is effective on a date other than a premium due date such that the policyholder has paid a premium for which he did not receive a full period of coverage.

33. Guaranteed renewable.

34. When the policyholder does not pay premiums, when the policyholder has engaged in fraud or misrepresentation, or when the insurer decides to stop offering the type of coverage provided by the policy.

35. Based on model laws and therefore somewhat uniform.

36. State insurance commissioners.

37. Recommends. (The NAIC has no power to force any state to adopt any law.)

38. May adopt them only in part or with modifications.

39. Their policies can adhere to these laws even with quite different wording and structure.

40. a. The Model Life and Health Insurance Policy Language Simplification Act.

   b. The Uniform Policy Provisions Law (UPPL).

   c. The Official Guide for Filing and Approval of Accident and Health Contracts.

   d. The Individual Accident and Sickness Insurance Minimum Standards Act.

41. Three years after an individual health insurance policy goes into effect, the insurer no longer has the right to rescind the policy because of misstatements in the application.

42. Fraud can be difficult to prove.

43. It limits an insurer's right to contest a policy to two years after the effective date.

44. Noncancellable and guaranteed renewable.

45. They limit to two years an insurer's right to refuse to provide coverage for preexisting conditions except for any that are specifically excluded by name.

46. It sets forth the procedure by which the policyholder can apply for reinstatement of the policy and the insurer can re-evaluate the risk of insuring him.

47. That illnesses that begin 10 days or less after reinstatement will not be covered.

48. 20 days.

49. 15 days.

50. 90 days.

51. 60 days.

52. It protects the insurer against lawsuits begun before it has had a reasonable opportunity to investigate a claim.

53. Three.

54. Provisions that state laws generally allow, but do not require, an insurer to include in individual medical expense insurance policies.

55. a. If the insured changes to an occupation that is more or less hazardous than her occupation at the time the policy was issued, the amount of premium is adjusted.

b. An unpaid premium can be deducted from claim payments.

c. The benefit amount is adjusted to what the premium paid would have purchased if the insured's correct age had been given.

56. • A schedule of benefits (making benefit provisions clear and easily understandable);

• the right of examination (allowing a policyholder to change his mind even after purchasing a policy); and

• model laws incorporating consistent and fair standards.

Answers to Practice Exam Questions

1. d

2. a

3. c

4. c

11 SALES OF GROUP HEALTH INSURANCE PRODUCTS

Introduction (Page 89)

✦ 1. What is meant by an insurer's **products**?

Participants in Group Insurance Sales (Pages 89–90)

✦ 2. What is an insurance **agent**?

3. Most agents work (under a contract with an insurer / as employees of an agency / as employees of an insurer).

4. Agents contract (with many different insurers / exclusively with one insurer / either).

5. Agents are usually compensated by (salary / commissions).

✦ 6. What is the common (though not entirely accurate) distinction made between agents and **brokers**?

7. Carl is a broker. He decides that the policy that best meets the needs of his client, Alta Company, is one offered by Northumberland Insurance. When Carl sells the policy to Alta, he is acting as the representative of (Alta / Northumberland).

8. In the above case, how will Carl probably be compensated?

9. (Agents only / Brokers only / Both agents and brokers / Neither agents nor brokers) are licensed by the state.

✦ 10. What are **employee benefit consultants**?

11. What is the distinction usually made between brokers and employee benefit consultants?

12. How are consultants compensated?

✦ 13. What are **group representatives**?

14. Group representatives deal with (sales only / service only / both sales and service).

Home Office and Field Offices (Page 91)

✦ 15. What is the **home office** of an insurance company?

✦ 16. What are **field sales offices**?

17. How do the responsibilities of home office and field office sales personnel differ?

The Sales Process for Group Health Insurance (Pages 91–94)

♦ 18. What is **prospecting**?

♦ 19. What is a **prospect**?

20. Prospecting is usually done by (agents and brokers / group representatives).

21. Normally, what is a group representative's role in prospecting?

♦ 22. What is a **request for proposals (RFP)**?

23. The decision to proceed to the stage of plan design and proposal preparation is made by the (home office / group representative).

24. A group representative bases her recommendation to proceed to the plan design stage on two main criteria. What are they?

25. Plan design typically involves (home office personnel / the group representative / both).

26. What tasks are involved in plan design?

27. What kinds of information are needed to design a plan?

♦ 28. What are **plan specifications**?

29. What is the purpose of plan specifications?

30. The preparation of a sales proposal involves (home office personnel / the group representative / both).

31. What are the three major kinds of information included in a sales proposal?

♦ 32. What does **cost illustration** do?

33. Why are cost illustrations usually not made for smaller groups?

34. A proposal is usually presented to a prospect by (the insurer's group representatives / the prospect's broker / both).

35. What are the two main areas a prospect considers in evaluating a proposal?

36. What is generally required to close a sale?

37. What are the two reasons that enrollment of employees is necessary?

38. Helstad Insurance is taking over the existing health insurance plan of HDD, Inc. The plan will remain the same except that vision care coverage is being added. Will HDD's employees need to be reenrolled?

39. Jutland Insurance is taking over the existing health insurance plan of Fiord Card Company. Benefits will stay the same, but the employee contribution to premiums will increase. Will Fiord's employees need to be reenrolled?

40. In cases where reenrollment is not strictly necessary, why might an insurer want to conduct it anyway?

41. What is the role of employer personnel in enrollment?

♦ 42. What is meant by the **installation** of a plan?

43. What are the responsibilities of the group representative in installation?

44. For small and medium-size groups, the group representative sometimes does not take responsibility for installation. Who does?

45. A group representative uses a check-off form in providing administrative assistance and continuing service. What are the uses of this form?

46. For small and medium-size groups, the group representative sometimes does not take responsibility for providing administrative assistance and continuing service. Who does?

47. From a business standpoint, what is the advantage of providing good service?

48. Sylvia, a group representative, works hard to maintain a close relationship and good communication with Donegal Dishes, a group policyholder. How will this help Sylvia keep Donegal's business?

49. How does her relationship with Donegal help Sylvia gain new business?

Agents and Brokers (Pages 94–95)

50. Some insurers are too small to employ group representatives. How do they sell and service policies?

♦ 51. What is a **direct writer** (in the context of sales)?

♦ 52. What is a **third-party administrator (TPA)**?

53. What type of insurance plans most commonly use third-party administrators?

54. Most sales of health insurance for small and medium-size groups are made by (agents / brokers).

55. Most sales of health insurance for large groups are made by (agents / brokers).

56. In the large group market, individual brokers and small general brokerage firms account for a (significant / insignificant) portion of sales.

57. In the large group market, who controls the largest percentage of the business in terms of premiums paid?

58. What advantage do large general brokerage firms have in the large group market?

59. What advantages does selling group health insurance give an agent?

60. (Group / Individual) agents have a work schedule close to a normal nine-to-five workday.

The Role of the Group Representative (Page 96)

61. What are the main sales responsibilities of a group representative?

62. Group representatives (sometimes / usually / always) contact prospects through agents and brokers.

63. What are the major service responsibilities that may be handled by the group representative?

64. In some companies another person is given the service responsibilities of the group representative. Who is this person?

65. What is the group representative's purpose in working with agents and brokers?

66. What activities does the group representative engage in with full-time agents of the insurer?

67. Why is a close working relationship between the group representative and the agent important?

68. How is a group representative's relationship with independent agents and brokers the same as her relationship with full-time agents of the insurer?

69. What is the group representative's focus in dealing with large, specialized brokerage firms and employee benefit consultants?

Summary (Page 97)

70. What are the seven steps of selling group health insurance?

Practice Exam Questions

1. The main distinction between brokers and employee benefit consultants is that, usually,

   a. brokers work with agents while consultants work alone.

   b. consultants only recommend policies while brokers also assist in the sale.

   c. consultants represent insurers while brokers represent policyholders.

   d. consultants work with large groups while brokers do not.

2. A request for proposals (RFP) is issued by an

   a. agent.

   b. employer.

   c. individual.

   d. insurer.

3. Which of the following is included in sales proposals for large groups but omitted for small groups?

   a. A cost illustration for the policy.

   b. A list of well-known group policyholders of the insurer.

   c. Information on the financial strength of the insurer.

   d. Premium rates for each coverage provided.

4. What kind of health plans most commonly use third-party administrators?

   a. Blue Cross/Blue Shield plans.

   b. Self-insured plans.

   c. Very large group plans.

   d. Very small group plans.

Answers

1. Insurance policies.

2. A person who acts for an insurer by selling its products and otherwise representing it.

3. Under a contract with an insurer.

4. Either.

5. Commissions.

6. An agent represents the insurer, and a broker represents the prospective policyholder.

7. Northumberland.

8. By a commission from Northumberland, although he may receive a fee from Alta for advising and assisting it.

9. Both agents and brokers.

10. Individuals or firms that specialize in group benefit plans for employees.

11. A broker assists his client in purchasing a policy, while most consultants focus on making recommendations to the client, which the client may then act on.

12. They receive a fee from the employers they advise.

13. Insurance company employees responsible for the selling and servicing of group insurance plans.

14. Either sales only or both sales and service, depending on whether the company also has group service representatives.

15. The headquarters of the company.

16. Offices established away from the home office so that salespeople can be closer to customers.

17. In general, the field sales personnel are directly involved in selling, and the home

office sales personnel support the field office personnel.

18. Identifying prospects and making initial contact with them.

19. A potential policyholder.

20. Agents and brokers.

21. Informing, motivating, and supporting agents and brokers.

22. A document issued by an employer notifying insurers that the employer is seeking coverage and inviting them to propose a plan.

23. The home office (although the recommendation of the group representative is important).

24. The prospect meets the insurer's underwriting standards, and there is a reasonably good chance of making the sale.

25. Both.

26. Evaluating the prospect's needs, designing a plan to meet those needs, underwriting the plan, and calculating the premium rates.

27. An employee census; a description of any present policy; the claims and premium experience of the present policy; and information on the business of the prospect, any hazards particular to its activities, the prospect's objectives and financial condition, and any collective bargaining agreements affecting the coverage.

28. Requirements for a health insurance plan set by the prospect.

29. To ensure that all proposals submitted have certain points in common so that the prospect can make direct comparisons.

30. Both.

31. • A brief description of each coverage offered in the plan;

   • the premium rates for each coverage; and

   • information on the insurer (its financial strength and accomplishments and a list of well-known group policyholders).

32. It shows what portion of the premium paid is used to pay benefits, expenses, etc., and how much, if any, may be returned to the policyholder as an experience refund.

33. Smaller groups are not eligible for experience refunds.

34. The broker.

35. The specifics of the plan design (such as benefits, premium rates, and cost illustration) and the insurer's capabilities, experience, and reputation.

36. The prospect must sign the application and pay the first month's premium.

37. To determine whether a sufficient number of employees will participate, and for record keeping.

38. Yes, so that they can be enrolled in the new coverage.

39. Yes. They must be given the option of participating under the new terms or not, and it must be determined if a sufficient number of employees will participate.

40. To help increase employee awareness of the plan and to introduce itself as the new insurer.

41. They distribute information, arrange for employee presentation meetings, distribute enrollment cards, and follow up to obtain the signed cards.

42. The plan goes into effect.

43. Delivering administrative material to the policyholder, reviewing the plan's administration, and establishing administrative procedures.

44. The agent.

45. Making a thorough review of administrative practices, tracking the status of various aspects of the plan, and serving as a report to the home office.

46. The agent.

47. The retention of business.

48. Sylvia will be aware of any problems that Donegal has and will be able to address them. Otherwise Donegal might respond to these problems by letting its policy lapse or transferring it to another insurer.

49. She has the opportunity to sell expanded or additional group coverages to Donegal.

50. They usually delegate all sales and service responsibilities to contracted agents and brokers.

51. An insurer that does not use agents or brokers at all and approaches prospective

policyholders only through its group representatives.

52. A firm that is neither the insurer nor the policyholder of a group insurance plan that takes responsibility for the administration of that plan.

53. Self-insured plans.

54. Agents.

55. Brokers.

56. Significant.

57. Brokers specializing in group health insurance and very large general brokerage firms with specialized group health insurance departments.

58. They already serve as advisors to the top management of large companies on other insurance lines (property, casualty, and fire), which gives them contacts in these companies and knowledge of the companies' operations and needs.

59. He makes contact with prospects for other business insurance or individual insurance. And if he is already selling other coverages to business clients, adding group health insurance enables him to offer a complete range of products and service to this market.

60. Group agents. (Individual agents must sell when individuals are at home.)

61. • Prospecting (usually through agents and brokers);

• submitting information about prospects to the home office and making recommendations on proposals;

• preparing proposals and presenting them to prospects;

• assisting in the closing of sales; and

• keeping the home office informed of competitive developments in the field.

62. Usually, but not always. (They may contact large employers directly.)

63. • Assisting in the enrollment of employees;

• installing the plan and setting up administrative procedures;

• making regular service calls to assist the employer in the administration of the policy and in insurance plan modernization; and

• retaining present policyholders by providing good service and maintaining good communication.

64. The group service representative.

65. To get them to bring business to the insurer.

66. Providing them with information, training them, and motivating them to prospect. This involves distributing written information, conducting training sessions, and organizing periodic meetings.

67. It is the most effective way for the group representative to educate and motivate the agent.

68. In both cases, the group representative's purpose is to get them to bring business to the insurer, and in both cases she works to inform, train, and motivate them and to establish close relationships with them.

69. Demonstrating his own abilities to the broker and convincing him of the superior products and capabilities of his company.

70. • Identifying prospects and making initial contact with them;

• designing a health insurance plan to meet the prospect's needs and packaging this plan into a proposal;

• presenting the proposal;

• closing the sale;

• enrolling the group members in the plan;

• executing the contract and installing the plan; and

• providing continuing service to the policyholder and the insureds.

Answers to Practice Exam Questions

1. b
2. b
3. a
4. b

12 SALES OF INDIVIDUAL HEALTH INSURANCE PRODUCTS

Introduction (Page 99)

1. The selling of individual health insurance is done largely by (insurer employees / agents and brokers).

2. What is the main difference between the work of agents and brokers selling group health insurance and that of those selling individual policies?

Agents and Brokers (Pages 99–100)

◆ 3. What is **field underwriting**?

4. How is field underwriting done?

5. What are the service responsibilities of individual agents?

6. What are the public relations responsibilities of individual agents?

7. What is the role of the individual broker?

8. When an individual broker sells a policy, she is serving as a representative of (the policyholder / the insurer).

9. Individual brokers are paid by (the policyholder / the insurer).

10. Brokers who sell individual health insurance policies usually sell (other types of insurance as well / only health insurance).

11. Why do some health insurers refuse to accept business from individual brokers?

12. How have large property and casualty brokerage firms addressed this situation?

Sales Offices and Agencies (Pages 100–101)

13. An insurer's branch office is (under the exclusive control of the insurer / an independent business under contract).

14. Who is in charge of an insurer's branch office?

15. What are the main responsibilities of the branch sales manager?

◆ 16. What is a **general agent**?

◆ 17. What is a **general agency**?

18. The facilities and staff of a general agency are provided by (the general agent / an insurer).

19. The agents of a general agency are recruited and supervised by (the general agent / an insurer).

20. What expenses of a general agency does an insurer sometimes help pay?

◆ 21. What is a **personal producing general agent (PPGA)**?

22. Most PPGAs (have / do not have) the authority to hire or appoint their own agents and work with brokers.

23. PPGAs usually (are responsible for their own expenses / rely on insurers for operating expense).

The Sales Process for Individual Health Insurance
(Pages 101–104)

24. What distinguishes a true prospect from a name?

25. Where does an agent get the names from which she develops a file of true prospects?

26. Why are present policyholders considered possible prospects?

27. How do agents reach prospects in specific professional or ethnic groups?

28. How do agents benefit from mass marketing methods?

◆ 29. What is the **approach**?

30. What are four approach methods?

◆ 31. What is a **cold call**?

◆ 32. How does a **pre-approach letter** work?

33. How can a pre-approach letter be combined with a referral?

◆ 34. **Centers of influence** are clients who have contact with many persons who respect their opinions. What are some examples?

35. What is the outcome of a successful approach?

36. What is an agent's purpose in an interview?

37. In an interview, an agent wants to know the answers to two questions. What are they?

38. What are the three categories of prospects' needs?

39. What does someone in the primary permanent category need?

◆ 40. What is a **primary health insurance policy**?

41. What does someone in the primary interim category need?

42. What does someone in the supplemental category need?

43. Give the need category for each of the following prospects:

    a. Susan has just graduated from college and is looking for her first fulltime job. She has no health insurance.

    b. Edward is 35 and self-employed. He is not covered by an employer's group plan or a government program and does not expect to be covered by either in the near future. He does not have an individual health insurance policy.

    c. Kyle has just been hired by Source Corporation and will be eligible for its group health insurance plan in six months. He is no longer covered by his previous group policy.

    d. Wanda is covered by her employer's group health plan, but it does not provide benefits for long-term care.

44. Most primary interim prospects will be covered by an employer's group plan within (one to six / six to 12 / 12 to 24) months.

45. What coverage will an agent most likely propose for each need category?

    a. Primary permanent.

    b. Primary interim.

    c. Supplemental.

46. How does the insurer assist the agent in presenting the recommended coverage?

47. In the presentation, the agent provides the prospect with the information he needs to decide whether to purchase the coverage. What is this information?

48. What is usually required to close a sale?

49. An agent typically has an orientation meeting with the policyholder when the policy goes into effect. What does the agent do in this meeting?

50. In what three ways does providing efficient service to a policyholder and maintaining a good relationship with him benefit an agent?

Direct Sales of Individual Health Insurance (Page 104)

◆ 51. What is meant by **direct sales** of health insurance products?

52. What kind of individual health insurance products are most commonly sold directly?

53. What single health insurance product is most commonly sold directly?

54. Mass marketing most often results in (direct sales / agent involvement).

Summary (Pages 104–105)

55. What are the seven steps of the individual sales process?

Practice Exam Questions

1. In individual health insurance, which of these does a branch sales manager usually <u>not</u> do?

   a. Contact prospects.

   b. Handle policyholders' service problems.

   c. Recruit agents.

   d. Train agents.

2. A personal producing general agent (PPGA) is a(n)

   a. consultant working for employers and associations.

   b. employee of an insurer.

   c. independent businessperson contracted to an insurer.

   d. independent businessperson not contracted to any insurer.

3. What is the result of a successful approach?

   a. An interview.

   b. A referral.

   c. A sale.

   d. The identification of a true prospect.

Answers

1. Agents and brokers.

2. Individual agents and brokers must deal person-to-person with many individuals.

3. Initial risk selection done by agents.

4. Agents make preliminary rough judgments about whether and on what terms the insurer would want to insure an individual.

5. Agents provide service to existing policyholders, including answering questions and assisting in policy changes.

6. Agents are responsible for projecting the proper image of the insurer to the consumer.

7. Assisting the prospective policyholder in finding a policy and insurer that offer the proper coverage at the best price.

8. The insurer.

9. The insurer.

10. Other types of insurance as well.

11. They maintain that since brokers often sell many types of coverage, they do not have the expertise in health insurance they need to provide both knowledgeable service to the consumer and field underwriting assistance to the insurer.

12. They have established separate departments staffed by brokers specializing in life and health insurance.

13. Under the exclusive control of the insurer.

14. A branch sales manager.

15. • Working with agents on sales;

    • recruiting and training new agents;

    • handling policyholders' service problems;

    • supervising office employees; and

    • managing the expenses of the office.

16. An independent businessperson who operates her own sales office under contract to an insurer.

17. The sales office of a general agent.

18. The general agent.

19. The general agent.

20. Overhead and the training and financing of new agents.

21. PPGAs, like general agents, are independent businesspersons under contract to an insurer. PPGAs are usually people who, having been successful agents for a number of years, seek contractual relationships that give them, in return for this ability to produce business, greater commission compensation than they received as agents.

22. Have.

23. Are responsible for their own expenses.

24. A true prospect is a potential policyholder, which means he must have a current need for health insurance, be able to pay for it, and be able to meet the insurer's underwriting requirements.

25. • Her friends, relatives, and acquaintances;

    • her present policyholders and those of the insurer she works for;

    • referrals from all of these people and from others;

    • telephone directories, city and county records, mortgage lists, graduation lists, announcements of marriages and births, and community activity lists; and

    • specialized lists from listing companies.

26. They can be sold additional coverages.

27. Through trade shows, newsletters, and the sponsorship of events targeted to these groups.

28. Prospects identified by insurer's mass marketing efforts are usually referred to an agent.

29. The first contact and attempt to set up an interview.

30. The cold call, the telephone call, the pre-approach letter, and the referral.

31. An unannounced visit by the agent to the prospect.

32. An agent sends a letter to the prospect to attempt to create interest in an interview and then follows up with a visit or telephone call to arrange the interview.

33. The letter contains a list of people (usually clients) who recommend the agent and are known to the prospect.

34. Attorneys, bankers, accountants, and realtors.

35. An interview.

36. To learn about the prospect's needs so that an appropriate policy can be recommended.

37. • What health insurance does the prospect already have?

    • Are there any gaps in that health insurance that need to be filled to ensure adequate protection?

38. Primary permanent, primary interim, and supplemental.

39. A primary health insurance policy on a permanent basis.

40. The policyholder's main health insurance coverage (not a supplement to another policy).

41. A primary policy but on a temporary basis.

42. Supplemental coverage to cover deficiencies in her primary policy.

43. a. Primary interim.

    b. Primary permanent.

    c. Primary interim.

    d. Supplemental.

44. One to six months.

45. a. Major medical expense coverage, disability income coverage, and perhaps long-term care coverage.

    b. The same as for primary permanent, but on a temporary basis.

c. A supplemental policy that fills the gaps in the prospect's current coverage.

46. The insurer prepares promotional material such as brochures, pamphlets, and visual aides.

47. The benefits and limitations of the coverage and how it meets the prospect's needs.

48. A signed application and a prepayment of the first premium.

49. She reviews the benefits the policy provides, explains the procedure for submitting a claim, and gives the policyholder a claim form. She may also hand-deliver the new policy.

50. • The policyholder is more likely to keep the policy.

   • The policyholder may give the agent referrals of new prospects.

   • The agent may be able to sell additional coverage to the policyholder.

51. The insurer sells coverages directly to consumers, without working through agents or brokers.

52. Supplemental coverages.

53. Travel accident insurance.

54. Agent involvement.

55. • Prospecting;

   • making the approach;

   • conducting the interview;

   • choosing a coverage to meet the needs of the prospect;

   • presenting the recommended coverage to the prospect;

   • closing the sale; and

   • providing service to the policyholder.

Answers to Practice Exam Questions

1. a
2. c
3. a

13 SALES COMPENSATION

Commissions (Pages 107–109)

 1. What is a **sales commission**?

2. Insurers compensate agents and brokers principally by (commissions / salaries / bonuses).

3. In insurance, how is the amount of a commission usually determined?

4. In individual sales, the percentage an agent receives in commission usually is (different / the same) for different premium amounts.

5. In group sales, the percentage an agent receives in commission usually is (different / the same) for different premium amounts.

6. In group sales, how are the commission percentages for different premium amounts determined?

7. An agent's commission is a percentage of premiums paid (during the initial term of the policy only / during both the initial term and following years if the contract is renewed).

8. Ellen is an insurance agent. She was ill this year and made very few sales. Nevertheless, she earned a substantial income in commissions. How is this possible?

9. What is a **high-low commission schedule**?

10. What is a **level commission schedule**?

11. In the long term, an agent generally earns (more with the high-low schedule / more with the level schedule / about the same with either).

12. Agents are allowed to choose the type of schedule by (all / some / no) insurers.

13. How does a high-low commission schedule affect insurer expenses?

14. A (level / high-low) schedule gives agents incentives to retain policyholders.

15. A (level / high-low) schedule gives agents incentives to replace policies.

16. Some insurers and the regulators in some states require a level schedule for group policies in five circumstances. What are these circumstances?

17. In general, the (high-low / level) commission schedule is becoming the more common schedule.

18. Most insurers pay higher commission percentages for (disability income insurance / medical expense insurance).

19. Insurers generally make more on (disability income insurance / medical expense insurance).

◆ 20. What is **persistency**?

21. (Disability income policies / Medical expense policies) have better persistency.

22. Why must agents usually devote more time to selling a disability income policy than a medical expense policy?

23. How do some insurers give agents an advance?

24. Why do some insurers pay a slightly higher commission scale for groups of fewer than 25 employees?

◆ 25. What is a **persistency fee**?

26. How can each of the following factors affect the commission percentage?

    a. The type of coverage sold.

    b. The length of time the policy has been in force.

    c. The size of the group.

    d. The amount of the premiums.

Override Commissions (Page 110)

◆ 27. An **override commission** is paid to (the agent making the sale / a general agent or agency manager).

28. What is the purpose of an override commission?

29. An override commission is based on (a high-low schedule / a level schedule / either).

Vesting (Pages 110–111)

◆ 30. What is **vesting**?

31. Nora, an agent, sells a policy for Archimedes Insurance. The policy is renewed each year, and Nora continues to receive commissions from it. After five years, Nora decides to leave Archimedes to work for another insurer. Her contract with Archimedes gives her vesting rights. Nora (will / will not) continue to receive commissions for the policy.

32. If Nora's contract with Archimedes does not give her vesting rights, she (will / will not) continue to receive commissions for the policy.

33. In what two ways does vesting differ among insurers?

34. If vesting is conditional, what do the conditions usually relate to?

35. Can an agent's estate receive commissions after her death?

36. The trend in group insurance is toward (more / less) vesting.

Other Compensation for Agents (Page 111)

37. Why may the income of new agents be low in the first few years?

38. How do some insurers financially assist new agents?

39. Advances are usually provided (to all agents selling for the insurer/ only to agents selling exclusively for the insurer).

40. What must a new agent generally do to qualify for a training allowance?

41. What fringe benefits do insurers typically provide to agents?

42. What must an agent generally do to be eligible for fringe benefits?

43. What extra incentives do insurers sometimes offer for high sales?

44. In addition to the financial compensation, how do incentives help motivate sales personnel?

Broker Fees (Page 112)

45. Some brokers of (individual coverage / group coverage) receive fees from the policyholders they assist.

46. Most brokers derive their income principally from (sales commissions paid by insurers / fees paid by policyholders).

47. Fees paid by employers to group brokers are usually (based on premiums / a flat monthly or annual amounts / a per-employee-per-month charge).

48. Fees are most common with brokers (representing large clients / representing small clients / acting as third-party administrators).

Bonuses for Insurer Employees (Page 112)

49. Group representatives sometimes receive incentive bonuses. For what?

50. Usually, group representatives are compensated primarily by (salary / commissions / bonus).

51. Group representative bonuses are usually (a percentage of premiums / a flat fee).

52. Branch sales managers usually receive compensation in addition to their salary. What is this additional compensation based on?

Practice Exam Questions

1. Is the sales commission percentage generally different for policies with different premium amounts, or is the percentage the same regardless of the amount of the premium?

   a. For both group and individual policies, the percentage is different for policies with different premium amounts.

   b. For both group and individual policies, the percentage is the same regardless of the size of the premium.

   c. For group policies the percentage is different for policies with different premium amounts, but for individual policies the percentage is the same regardless of the size of the premium.

   d. For individual policies the percentage is different for policies with different premium amounts, but for group policies the percentage is the same regardless of the size of the premium.

2. What contract provision allows an agent to collect commissions from an insurer that she no longer works for?

   a. High-low commission schedule.

   b. Level commission schedule.

   c. Override commissions.

   d. Vesting of commissions.

3. Which statement is correct about the high-low commission schedule?

   a. It allows agents to earn more in the long run.

   b. It encourages agents to replace policies.

   c. It is the most common commission schedule.

   d. Regulators require it in some circumstances.

4. The earnings of brokers of individual health insurance usually consist of

   a. commissions from insurers, not fees from policyholders.

   b. fees from policyholders, not commissions from insurers.

   c. a combination of fees and commissions.

   d. some fees and commissions, but mostly salary and bonuses from an insurer.

Answers

1. A payment made to a salesperson for the sale of a product.

2. Commissions.

3. The commission that an agent receives for the sale of a policy is normally a percentage of the premiums the policyholder pays on that policy.

4. The same.

5. Different.

6. They are set by a commission schedule.

7. During both the initial term and following years if the contract is renewed.

8. She earned commissions from policies sold in previous years and still in force.

9. A schedule that pays the agent a higher percentage of premiums during the first year a policy is in force and lower commissions in renewal years.

10. A schedule that pays the same percentage every year.

11. About the same with either.

12. Some.

13. A high-low schedule adds to an insurer's first-year expenses, which are already high.

14. Level. (The level schedule gives agents greater compensation for renewals.)

15. High-low. (If policies are replaced, the agent earns a first-year commission.)

16. • A group coverage is being transferred from one insurer to another.

    • A group policy is being reinstated.

    • The group policyholder is not contributing to premiums.

    • A group policy is judged by the insurer to have a high chance of lapse.

    • An employer's group policy is negotiated with unions.

17. Level.

18. Disability income insurance.

19. Disability income insurance.

20. The likelihood that the policyholder will renew the policy year after year.

21. Disability income policies.

22. Persuading consumers of the need for income protection and arriving at the proper amount of coverage can be time-consuming.

23. By paying the commissions for all of the first-year premiums in one sum as soon after the sale as possible, instead of waiting until the premiums are actually paid.

24. For small groups the agent often does more of the work of selling, installing, and servicing.

25. A fee paid by some insurers to the agent if a policy remains in force beyond the tenth policy year.

26. a. Percentages are higher for disability income insurance than for medical expense insurance.

    b. Percentages will vary with time if a high-low schedule and/or persistency payments apply.

    c. Higher percentages may be paid for smaller groups.

    d. The percentage will vary with the premium amount for group policies, but not for individual policies.

27. A general agent or agency manager.

28. It compensates this person for the assistance he provides to the selling agent.

29. Either.

30. The right of an agent to receive commissions payable from an insurance sale even after termination of her contract with the insurer.

31. Will.

32. Will not.

33. Some companies pay all of the commission, while others pay only a portion; some companies give unconditional vesting rights, while others grant vesting only under certain conditions.

34. How long the agent has been with the insurer, the amount of the agent's sales, and the reason for the agent's termination (such as whether the termination was voluntary or

involuntary, or if it was due to death or disability).

35. Yes (depending on the agent's contract).

36. Less.

37. New agents have not had the time to develop a base of prospects, and they are not receiving renewal commissions from sales made in previous years.

38. By paying them advances on future commissions and/or by paying them a training allowance (a salary).

39. Only to agents selling exclusively for the insurer.

40. Produce a certain amount of premiums or commissions.

41. A group health and life insurance plan, a retirement plan, and the insurer's Social Security program.

42. She must be working full-time for the insurer and must habitually produce a certain amount of business.

43. Specified monetary awards and trips to sales conventions.

44. Through the recognition of excellence.

45. Group coverage.

46. Commissions.

47. A flat monthly or annual amounts or a per-employee-per-month charge.

48. Representing large clients or acting as third-party administrators.

49. Exceeding goals or quotas.

50. Salary.

51. A percentage of premiums.

52. The quantity and quality of sales, the retention of business, and/or the amount of premium that policyholders continue to pay year after year.

Answers to Practice Exam Questions

1. c

2. d

3. b

4. a

14 MARKETING OF HEALTH INSURANCE PRODUCTS

Introduction (Pages 113–114)

1. How has the use of the term **marketing** changed?

2. What are the four broad areas of marketing?

3. In a health insurance company, what are the four marketing functions?

4. In what way are all corporate functions directly or indirectly related to marketing?

5. What are **actuaries**?

6. What do actuaries do?

7. How can the following people affect product sales or the retention of a policyholder?

   a. Actuaries.

   b. Customer service personnel.

   c. Claims personnel.

Markets for Group Health Insurance Products (Pages 114–116)

8. What two criteria do insurers use to divide the market for group health insurance into smaller market segments?

9. What is a **single employer** (in the context of health insurance)?

10. A single employer is most commonly a (sole proprietor / partnership / corporation).

11. Bering Books, Atlantic Publishing, and Charon Design are each a separate legal entity, but all are subsidiary companies owned by Marengo Corporation. Marengo procures insurance for all three companies. The policyholder in this case (is / is not) considered to be a single employer.

12. Single employers account for about (50 / 70 / 90) percent all group policies in force.

13. How are **Multiple-Employer Trusts (METs)** formed?

14. In the case of a multiple employer trust, the policyholder is (each employer / the trust).

15. What are the advantages of a multiple employer trust?

16. **Trade associations** are groups of (companies / individuals).

17. How are trade associations involved in health insurance?

18. In trade association arrangements, the policyholder is (each company / each individual / the association).

19. Trade association arrangements account for a (considerable / very small) portion of all group contracts in force.

◆ 20. **Professional associations** are groups of (companies / individuals).

21. How are professional associations and other individual associations involved in health insurance?

22. Policies issued to a professional association (may cover only association members / sometimes cover both members and the employees of members).

23. In individual association arrangements, (the association is the policyholder and pays the premium / the individual is the policyholder and pays the premium / the association is the policyholder but the individual pays the premium).

24. Professional and other individual associations make up a (large / small) part of all group contracts in force.

25. How are labor unions involved in health insurance?

26. In labor union arrangements, premiums are paid by (the union from member dues / the individual member / the union and the individual member / any of these).

27. The number of group policies held by unions is (large but declining / small but growing / large and growing / small and declining).

28. What is the strategy that most unions adopt to obtain health insurance for their members?

◆ 29. How are negotiated **union-management trusteeships (Taft-Hartley groups)** involved in health insurance?

30. In a Taft-Hartley group arrangement, the policy is held by (the employers / the unions / a trusteeship).

31. Why may Taft-Hartley trusteeships only apply to union members engaged in activities that affect interstate or foreign commerce?

32. Taft-Hartley groups account for a (considerable / very small) part of all group insurance contracts in force.

33. How are creditor groups involved in health insurance?

34. Groups are categorized by size according to (the amount of premiums paid / the number of people insured).

◆ 35. What is meant by number of **insured lives**?

36. Which of the following sentences accurately describes how group size is usually defined for marketing purposes?

a. Small groups have fewer than 25 lives, medium-size groups have 25 to 50 lives, and large groups have more than 50 lives.

b. Small groups have fewer than 50 lives, medium-size groups have 50 to 100 lives, and large groups have more than 100 lives.

c. Small groups have fewer than 100 lives, medium-size groups have 100 to 500 lives, and large groups have more than 500 lives.

37. Which group size category does each of these sentences describe (small, medium-size, or large groups)?

a. This category accounts for a large majority (about 80 percent) of all group health insurance policies in force.

b. This category accounts for a small minority (about 10 percent) of all group health insurance policies in force.

c. This category accounts for more than half of total premium dollars paid.

d. Agents, brokers, and consultants all actively sell to this category.

e. The majority of sales to this category are made by agents.

f. The majority of sales to this category are made through brokers or employee benefit consultants.

g. Insurers sometimes sell to this category directly (not through agents or brokers).

h. In this category, policies and administrative procedures are often tailored to the specifications of the buyer.

i. In this category, policies are not tailored to each buyer but some flexibility in benefit design and administration can be offered.

38. What are the primary concerns of purchasers of insurance for small groups?

39. What are the primary concerns of purchasers of insurance for medium-size groups?

Markets for Individual Health Insurance Products (Page 116)

40. Insurers sell individual health insurance policies to three consumer groups that correspond to the three need categories discussed in Chapter 12. Describe the people of each group and state the corresponding need category.

Mass Marketing of Individual Insurance (Pages 116–118)

41. Insurers sell most individual health insurance policies through (agents and brokers / mass marketing).

42. What is the advantage of using mass marketing?

43. If a prospect responds to mass marketing, she is contacted and the sale is made by (an insurer employee / an agent / either).

44. What are the mass marketing techniques used in insurance sales?

◆ 45. How does **direct mail** work?

46. How can interested prospects respond to direct mail?

47. What characteristics must a policy have to be appropriate for advertising?

48. What two coverages are most often advertised?

49. How can interested prospects respond to newspaper and magazine advertising?

50. How can interested prospects respond to radio and television advertising?

◆ 51. In **third-party sponsorship**, what is the third party?

52. How does third-party sponsorship typically work?

53. If a customer of the third party buys a policy, the third party usually handles (all transactions related to the policy / none of the transactions related to the policy / billing but no other transactions).

◆ 54. **Franchise plans** are an approach to selling (group / individual) policies.

55. Franchise plans target (a group / separate individuals).

56. What is another name for franchise plans?

57. In franchise plans, the policyholder is (an individual / an employer or association).

58. In franchise plans, underwriting is done on (a group / an individual) basis.

59. If a standard policy is used in franchise plans, it (must apply to all members of the targeted group / can be modified for some members).

60. Franchise plans offer individuals who do not have access to group insurance some of the advantages of group insurance. What are these advantages?

61. How can insurers provide lower premium rates in policies sold by franchise plans?

62. In franchise plans, the premium is paid by the (employer / employee).

63. How do payroll deductions work in franchise plans?

64. How are premiums paid when the group is an association?

65. What groups typically do not have group insurance and so can benefit from franchise plans?

66. What are the advantages of franchise plans for insurers?

67. What are the advantages of franchise plans for an employer?

68. Under what circumstances might an insurer market a franchise plan to a group that has group health insurance?

69. Franchise plans provide coverage for (employees only / employees and dependents).

70. Franchise plan policies are generally (noncancellable / guaranteed renewable / nonrenewable for stated reasons only / optionally renewable).

71. What usually happens if someone insured under a franchise plan leaves the group?

72. What information is typically provided on insurer Internet sites?

Product Research and Development (Pages 119–121)

✦ 73. What are the purposes of **research and development (R&D)** activities?

74. Personnel involved in R&D tend to (be limited to the R&D department or committee / include people from various departments).

75. What is another name for the R&D department?

✦ 76. What does a **product development statement** do?

77. The product development process has seven stages. What are they?

78. What decision is made by project managers at the end of each stage?

79. On what is this decision based?

80. Who generates ideas for new products?

81. What are these ideas based on?

82. What does an insurer try to learn by doing market research?

83. What four things are clarified by a product outline?

84. What are some examples of target markets?

85. What five questions does a market analysis ask about a proposed product?

86. What six activities are involved in product design and development?

✦ 87. What is meant by **product introduction**?

88. How is a new product monitored and reviewed to determine how it is performing?

Trends in the Marketing of Health Insurance Products (Page 121)

✦ 89. What are **mandated benefits**?

90. What does the Financial Services Modernization Act of 1999 do?

91. What kinds of health insurance are most likely to lend themselves to the markets that financial services companies want to reach?

Summary (Pages 121–122)

92. In terms of marketing, on what two factors does the success and growth of an insurance company depend?

Practice Exam Questions

1. In which of the four marketing functions of insurance companies are actuaries most often involved?

   a. Identifying markets for the types of coverage the company sells.

   b. Researching the precise needs of people who might want to buy that coverage.

   c. Developing insurance policies that meet those needs.

   d. Promoting and selling those policies.

2. Most group health insurance policies are held by

   a. labor unions.

   b. multiple employer trusts.

   c. single employers.

   d. union-management trusteeships.

3. In health insurance sales, which statement describes the small group category?

   a. This category accounts for a majority of policies.

   b. This category accounts for a majority of premium dollars.

   c. Insurers often tailor policies to groups in this category.

   d. Insurers often sell directly to groups in this category.

4. In health insurance sales, how does a third-party sponsorship work?

   a. A broker, consultant, or some other third party arranges for several employers in the same or related industries to come together to purchase group health insurance.

   b. A trade association acts as a third party between its members and an insurer to facilitate the purchase of health insurance.

   c. An insurer markets health insurance products by inserting advertising in the correspondence of a third party such as a bank or credit card company.

   d. Several unions and employers create a trust, which acts as a third party to purchase group health insurance for employees, who are members of the unions.

Answers

1. In the past, it referred to the salesperson's sales plans and sales methods. It now refers to a wide range of functions performed by a variety of people.

2. • Identifying a market;

   • evaluating the needs of that market;

   • developing products to meet those needs; and

   • promoting and distributing those products.

3. • Identifying markets for the types of coverage the company sells;

   • researching the precise needs of people who might want to buy that coverage;

   • developing insurance policies that meet those needs; and

   • promoting and selling those policies.

4. Every activity that company employees engage in affects product and service quality and so ultimately helps determine whether consumers buy the company's products.

5. Insurance mathematicians.

6. They analyze numerical data to calculate premium rates, dividends, and reserves and to prepare statistical studies and reports.

7. a. They must make rates for new and existing products as competitive as possible while maintaining profitability.

   b. They can suggest premium-reducing options to policyholders who are considering renewal.

   c. They can reward policyholders for finding billing errors or reporting fraud.

8. The type of policyholder and the size of the insured group.

9. An employer that is a single legal entity that purchases group coverage for its employees.

10. Corporation.

11. Is.

12. 90 percent.

13. An insurer, agent, broker, consultant, or insurance administrator arranges for several employers, usually in the same or related industries, to come together and form a trust to purchase health insurance for their employees.

14. The trust.

15. It creates a large group of insureds, giving a group of small companies many of the same advantages as a single employer with a large number of employees, including lower premiums.

16. Companies.

17. Employers that are members of a trade association may provide insurance for their employees through the association.

18. The association.

19. Very small (less than 1 percent).

20. Individuals.

21. Members of an association can provide themselves with group coverage through a policy issued to the association or to a trust formed to administer the insurance.

22. Sometimes cover both members and the employees of members.

23. The association is the policyholder but the individual pays the premium.

24. Small.

25. Some labor unions purchase group policies to provide health insurance coverage for their members.

26. Any of these.

27. Small and declining.

28. They use collective bargaining to get employers to provide group health insurance.

29. Working within the framework of the Labor Management Relations Act of 1947 (the Taft-Hartley Act), one or more unions negotiate group health insurance coverage for their members with one or more employers.

30. A trusteeship.

31. Because the Taft-Hartley Act is a federal law, not a state law.

32. Very small (about 2 percent).

33. A lending institution may buy a policy to

insure itself against nonpayment by persons owing it money due to the death or disability of those persons.

34. The number of people insured.

35. The number of people insured.

36. c. (Small groups have less than 100 lives, medium-size groups have 100 to 500 lives, and large groups have more than 500 lives.)

37. a. Small groups.

   b. This is true of both medium-size and large groups.

   c. Large groups.

   d. Medium-size groups.

   e. Small groups.

   f. Large groups.

   g. Large groups.

   h. Large groups.

   i. Medium-size groups.

38. Cost, simplified administration, and getting the same kinds and quality of benefits that are available to larger groups.

39. Cost, flexibility of plan design, and quality of service.

40. • People who depend solely or largely on an individual policy for health insurance protection (need category: primary permanent);

   • people who need temporary coverage (need category: primary interim); and

   • people covered by a primary health insurance plan but needing supplemental coverage to meet deficiencies in their primary plan (need category: supplemental).

41. Agents and brokers.

42. An insurer can approach a large number of prospects cheaply and quickly.

43. Either.

44. Direct mail, advertising, third-party sponsorship, franchise plans, and the Internet.

45. An insurer targets prospects and sends them by mail a proposal describing the coverage it is offering.

46. They fill out a short-form application and mail it back to the insurer.

47. It must have limited, easy-to-understand benefits.

48. Hospital indemnity and limited medical expense coverage.

49. They fill out a short-form application contained in the advertisement and mail it back to the insurer.

50. They call a toll-free telephone number for additional information or to apply for the coverage.

51. A non-insurance business that provides an insurer with access to its customers.

52. The insurer sends advertisements with the third party's billing or correspondence, or places advertisements in the third party's place of business.

53. Billing but no other transactions.

54. Individual.

55. A group.

56. Worksite marketing.

57. Individual.

58. Individual.

59. Can be modified for some members.

60. A reduction in the premium rate and the convenience of paying premiums through payroll deductions.

61. Because of the volume of business the group offers and because of lower commissions paid to agents for such sales.

62. Employee.

63. The employer takes the money out of the policyholder's paycheck and passes it along to the insurer.

64. Members pay premiums to a designated person who pays the insurer.

65. Smaller firms, associations, and groups that do not meet the legal definition of a group eligible for group insurance under state insurance laws.

66. They are an effective and economical way to market and service individual insurance policies.

67. They are a way to attract and retain

employees by giving them the opportunity of acquiring health insurance, without the employer contributing to the cost.

68. When a group plan provides only basic coverage, an insurer can market supplemental coverages.

69. Employees and dependents.

70. Optionally renewable or guaranteed renewable.

71. He may not continue the same coverage, but very often can convert to a similar policy offered by the insurer.

72. Product information, rate quotes, and in some cases company comparisons.

73. To develop ideas for new products and improvements in existing products and to ensure that these innovations meet real consumer needs and support corporate goals.

74. Include people from various departments.

75. The product management department.

76. It defines the insurer's overall goals and strategy in developing new products. Specifically, it clarifies the financial objectives of product development efforts, the customers the insurer seeks to target, and the degree of financial risk the company is willing to undertake.

77. • Idea generation,

• market research,

• product outline,

• market analysis,

• product design and development,

• product introduction, and

• sales monitoring and review.

78. Whether the development project should proceed to the next stage.

79. Compatibility of the project with the insurer's product development statement as well as other factors such as resources available for the project and projections of profits from it.

80. Field sales personnel, home office staff, or senior management.

81. Perceptions of consumer needs.

82. If there is really a need for the proposed product and to what extent competitors are already meeting this need.

83. • Who the product is intended for;

• what characteristics differentiate the product from others;

• how much developing the product will cost; and

• what benefits will be derived from developing the product.

84. A group size and type, a geographic area, an industry, or a socioeconomic group.

85. • Is the product compatible with the insurer's product development statement?

• What expertise and ability will be required to develop the product?

• Will the product work well with the other products and services the insurer already sells in the market it services?

• Can the insurer's current distribution and administration systems handle the product?

• How will sale of the product be influenced by the other "players in the game" (consumers, providers of health care, the government, and competitors)?

86. • Creating the contract for the product and filing it with state insurance departments;

• developing premium rates and commission schedules;

• setting underwriting limits, requirements, and guidelines and creating underwriting manuals;

• developing sales training programs and materials;

• creating sales presentation materials; and

• modifying data processing systems and administrative processes.

87. The sales department presents the product to prospects and begins selling.

88. Through analysis of sales results, analysis of a number of quotes, and input from the insurer's sales staff and agents.

89. Recent federal and state laws requiring that certain coverages provide certain benefits.

90. It removes barriers between banking,

securities, and insurance, paving the way for greater marketing of insurance through financial holding companies.

91. Specialty coverages such as long-term care insurance.

92. The success of its marketing personnel in performing core marketing activities and the degree to which all personnel of the company see the ultimate purpose of their work as the attraction and retention of business.

Answers to Practice Exam Questions

1. c

2. c

3. a

4. c

15 UNDERWRITING OF GROUP HEALTH INSURANCE

Principles of Group Underwriting (Pages 124–125)

◆ 1. What is **underwriting**?

◆ 2. What are **terms of coverage**?

3. In group insurance, an offer is (almost always / sometimes / usually not) made.

4. The focus of group underwriting is deciding (whether to offer coverage / the terms of coverage to be offered.)

5. Why is underwriting based on prediction of claims?

6. What are the two main things that an underwriter must decide?

7. How are statistical averages used to predict a group's claims?

8. How are general characteristics used to predict a group's claims?

9. Most groups that an underwriter considers (are seeking insurance for the first time / already have insurance but want to change insurers).

10. How is actual claims experience of a group used to predict future claims?

◆ 11. What is **adverse selection**?

12. Why is adverse selection a concern in underwriting?

13. How does competition work to make terms more favorable to policyholders?

The Group Underwriting Process (Pages 126–127)

14. Where can underwriters find procedures and standards for the underwriting process?

15. Underwriting manuals are (standard for all insurers / issued by each insurer for its own use).

16. A group underwriter almost always offers coverage to a small group because (such groups are almost always acceptable risks / regulations do not usually allow the insurer to decline to offer coverage to such groups).

17. A group underwriter almost always offers coverage to a large group because (such groups are almost always acceptable risks / regulations do not usually allow the insurer to decline to offer coverage to such groups).

18. Why must an underwriter, in predicting claims, assume a tentative set of benefit provisions?

19. In the case of a new group, what benefits does the underwriter assume?

20. In the case of an existing group, what benefits does the underwriter assume?

21. If the underwriter is making a projection of claims based on statistical averages for similar groups, what must he do?

22. Where does the underwriter find statistical averages such as standard projections of claims and adjustments for group characteristics?

23. If the underwriter is making a projection of claims based on the group's actual claims experience, what must he do?

24. Whether underwriting is based on averages or experience, the underwriter must do two additional things. What are they?

25. The underwriter bases premium rates on (statistical averages / actual experience of the group / either or both).

26. Where does the underwriter find standard rates and adjustments for group characteristics?

27. Rates are (subject to state laws and regulations / determined solely by each insurer).

28. An underwriter sometimes suggests that the benefit provisions requested by a group be modified in the final contract. What is usually the reason?

29. How are underwriters involved in the renewal of a policy?

30. How are underwriters involved in the revision of a policy?

Large Groups and Small Groups (Pages 128–130)

31. For underwriting purposes, a small group is generally considered to be one with (25 / 50 / 100) or fewer insureds.

32. In deciding whether to base prediction of claims on the actual claims experience of the group being considered or on statistical averages, two principles must be taken into account. What are they?

33. If a small group is being underwritten, these two principles conflict. Why?

34. If a large group is being underwritten, there is no conflict between the two principles. Why not?

35. For large groups the level of claims (is usually roughly the same every year / fluctuates greatly from year to year).

36. For small groups the level of claims (is usually roughly the same every year / fluctuates greatly from year to year).

37. Why can the actual claims experience of a large group be used to project future claims of that group?

38. Why can the actual claims experience of a small group not be used to project future claims of that group?

39. Why are projections for small groups not as accurate as for large groups?

♦ 40. How does **experience pooling** work?

41. What problem does experience pooling address?

42. Why must claims projections for large groups be more accurate than for small groups?

43. Underwriters generally base the premium rates of small groups on (averages / actual claims experience of the group / both).

44. Underwriters generally base the premium rates of large groups on (averages / actual claims experience of the group / both).

45. Underwriters generally base the premium rates of medium-size groups on (averages / actual claims experience of the group / both).

46. If a group's level of claims turns out to be much lower than projected, what will an insurer sometimes do?

47. Why is adverse selection a particular concern with small groups?

48. How have HIPAA and many state laws affected the efforts of insurers to deal with the problem of adverse selection in small groups?

♦ 49. What is meant by **guaranteed issue**?

50. What laws require guaranteed issue?

51. Underwriting under guaranteed issue conditions (includes / does not include) deciding whether or not to offer coverage.

52. (Small groups / Large groups) have higher administrative costs per insured person.

53. How do insurers try to keep administrative costs down for small groups?

Declining to Offer Coverage (Page 131)

54. An underwriter will (often / rarely) recommend that the insurer not offer coverage to a group.

55. What are the four most common reasons an underwriter will recommend not offering coverage to a group?

56. Sometimes only a small proportion of the eligible members of a group enroll in a plan. Why would an underwriter possibly recommend not offering coverage in this situation?

♦ 57. What is a **fictitious group**?

58. Why would an insurer not offer coverage to a fictitious group?

59. Why does an insurer want a new group to continue coverage for a reasonable period?

♦ 60. What are **acquisition expenses**?

61. What costs are included in acquisition expenses?

62. What kinds of businesses are likely to continue coverage for only a short period?

Projecting Claims: Adjusting Averages for Group Characteristics (Pages 132–133)

63. What are the main general characteristics of groups used in underwriting?

64. In underwriting large groups, adjustments for group characteristics are not usually made. Why not?

65. (Older / Younger) people make more health insurance claims.

66. On what statistic are age adjustments based?

67. (Women / Men) generally make more health insurance claims.

68. (Women / Men) have a greater incidence of disabilities.

69. (Women / Men) have higher claims for accidental death and dismemberment insurance.

70. On what statistic are gender adjustments based?

71. Why does the proportion of a group's insureds who are dependents affect claims levels?

72. What are the factors that have caused recent changes in the traditional proportions of dependents?

73. How has the increase in working women changed dependent participation?

74. Benefits for illnesses and accidents resulting directly from a person's employment are generally provided by (health insurance / state workers' compensation programs).

75. Ailments that result indirectly from work activities or the physical environment of the workplace usually (are / are not) covered by group health insurance.

76. Conditions likely to indirectly cause health problems are more common in some kinds of businesses than in others. Underwriters (do / do not) take this into account.

77. In some cases, the environment or work activities typical of a certain kind of business do not indirectly cause health conditions, but nonetheless workers in that field are on average less healthy. Why?

78. Why might a group with a disproportionate number of high-income individuals have high claims?

79. Why might a group with a disproportionate number of low-income individuals have high claims?

80. In general, the geographical location of a group significantly affects (the number of claims made / the cost of claims / both).

81. Charges for medical care are generally higher in (urban / rural) areas.

82. What problem might a high average age of a group indicate?

83. What problem might a very low average age of a group indicate?

84. What two problems are caused by high turnover?

Projecting Claims: Examining a Group's Claims Experience (Pages 134–135)

85. If a large group has actual claims experience, underwriting will be based largely on (experience / averages).

86. If a small group has actual claims experience, underwriting will be based largely on (experience / averages).

87. Even when underwriting is to be based on averages, the underwriter should still examine the group's claims experience. Why?

88. Why do most groups seeking to change insurers do so?

89. Why should an underwriter try to determine the reason a group is seeking to change insurers?

90. If the underwriting of a group is to be based on past claims data, what is the underwriter's first task?

♦ 91. What is meant by **reliability of data**?

92. What are the two main considerations in determining if claims data are reliable?

93. For large groups, the level of claims (fluctuates widely from year to year / is roughly the same every year, but has significant fluctuations / does not fluctuate enough from year to year to have any practical consequences).

94. The (more / fewer) years of data that are available, the clearer the typical annual amount of claims will be.

95. If a high level of claims is the result of many small claims, it (will likely continue / may or may not continue).

96. If a high level of claims is the result of a few very large claims, it (will likely continue / may or may not continue).

97. What is an example of a large claim that is not likely to recur?

98. What is an example of a large claim that is likely to recur?

99. If a large claim is not considered likely to continue or recur, the underwriter (may disregard part of the claim / must include all of the claim) in projecting future claims.

100. If a large claim is considered likely to continue or recur, the underwriter (may disregard part of the claim / must include all of the claim) in projecting future claims.

101. Why is the completeness, accuracy, and reliability of past claims data of particular concern for very large groups?

102. Why does the underwriting of an existing group require more work than the underwriting of new groups?

103. In making decisions related to the evaluation of claims experience, what does an underwriter do if the insurer's established procedures do not provide a clear-cut answer?

Examining the Provisions of an Existing Plan (Pages 135–139)

104. When she is underwriting a group with an existing plan, the underwriter must review (the contract of the previous plan / a copy of the employee booklet or certificate of insurance / both / either).

105. Why does an underwriter try to obtain information about the present insurer's actions on renewal of the plan?

106. If there are provisions in an existing plan that differ significantly from the new insurer's standard contract, what must the underwriter do?

107. In group health insurance, different classes of employees of a business (must be eligible for coverage under one plan / may be covered under different plans).

108. In group health insurance, (all employees of a business must be covered / some classes may be provided with coverage and not others).

109. Why do insurers consider the inclusion of all permanent full-time employees in one plan the most desirable approach?

110. Why might hourly-paid employees and salaried (professional and managerial) employees have different health plans?

111. What is an insurer's main concern about a group made up of only salaried employees?

112. What is the potential for adverse selection if only executives and key personnel are covered by a plan?

113. Why do insurers prefer that part-time, seasonal, and temporary employees be covered by a separate plan?

◆ 114. What is a **minimum enrollment requirement**?

115. How do minimum enrollment requirements help prevent adverse selection?

116. Most group insurance contracts require that (50 / 75 / 90) percent of employees carry coverage for their dependents.

117. If dependent participation is low because many employees have spouses with coverage from their own employers, what might an insurer do?

118. In what situation related to dependent participation does the insurer run the risk of adverse selection?

♦ 119. The payment of premiums under a certain plan is **noncontributory.** This means that the (employee / employer) does not contribute to the cost.

♦ 120. The payment of premiums under a certain plan is **contributory.** This means that the (employee / employer) contributes to the cost.

121. Payment on a (noncontributory / contributory) basis ensures participation of all employees.

122. What three advantages does payment on a noncontributory basis have for the insurer?

123. Why is there no possibility of adverse selection in a noncontributory plan?

124. What administrative tasks are necessary in contributory plans but not in noncontributory plans?

♦ 125. A certain plan is **fully contributory.** This means that the (employee / employer) contributes all of the premium.

126. What disadvantages does fully contributory payment have for an insurer in each of these areas?

   a. Level of benefits.

   b. Level of participation.

   c. Maintaining participation.

   d. Administration.

127. How do insurers respond to these disadvantages?

128. Fully contributory plans are illegal in (all / some / no) states.

129. Why must an underwriter examine the benefit provisions of an existing plan?

130. Under what circumstances might an underwriter propose an expansion of benefits?

131. The underwriter should pay particular attention to existing plans in which the benefits are (minimal / very liberal / either).

132. How can minimal benefits be a problem?

133. Generally, the coordination of benefits provisions of group health insurance policies coordinate benefits with (other group policies / individual policies / both).

134. How can very liberal benefits be a problem in contributory plans?

135. In a very small group, what problem can liberal benefits present?

136. In terms of administration, what are generally the expectations of a policyholder that is transferring a plan?

137. How must the underwriter address the expectations of the policyholder?

138. Name three important administrative issues that may arise when a plan is transferred from one insurer to another.

◆ 139. What is **self-billing**?

◆ 140. What do **no loss-no gain regulations** require?

141. No loss-no gain regulations are (state / federal) regulations that apply to (group / individual / both group and individual) insurance.

142. What federal law also restricts exclusions of preexisting conditions when a group plan is transferred?

◆ 143. What are **extended benefits**?

144. Why must underwriters be aware of extended benefits provisions in an existing contract?

Setting Premium Rates for an Existing Plan (Page 139)

145. Generally, how does an insurer set rates for an existing large group?

146. How does an insurer set premium rates for an existing small group?

Underwriting and Managed Care (Page 139)

147. (Employers / Insurers / Both employers and insurers) have taken the initiative in shifting existing plans to managed care.

148. The shift to managed care has made underwriting (simpler / more complex).

149. What is the main task an underwriter must undertake when an existing plan shifts to managed care?

150. What information must an underwriter take into account if a plan's HMO or PPO is being replaced with another?

Information Sources for Group Underwriting (Pages 140–141)

151. What underwriting information is provided in a request for proposals (RFP) and accompanying forms?

152. What employee data is usually included in an RFP?

153. Why is an employer's prior insurance history important to an underwriter?

154. What information is usually provided on enrollment cards?

155. Insurers use commercial investigating companies for (large / small) groups.

156. What do representatives of commercial investigating companies do?

157. What reporting requirements of the Employee Retirement Income Security Act (ERISA) are relevant to underwriting?

158. The above-mentioned reporting requirements of ERISA apply to (large / small) employers.

159. What other sources of underwriting information are there in addition to RFPs, enrollment cards, inspection reports, and ERISA reports?

Summary (Page 141)

160. What happens if an underwriter's projections are too high?

161. What happens if an underwriter's projections are too low?

Practice Exam Questions

1. If adverse selection occurs in a group, the claims level of the group will

   a. be unaffected.

   b. decrease.

   c. increase.

   d. move closer to the average.

2. Group underwriters

   a. almost always offer coverage to large groups, but often decline to offer coverage to small groups.

   b. almost always offer coverage to small groups, but often decline to offer coverage to large groups.

   c. almost always offer coverage to both large and small groups.

   d. often decline to offer coverage to both large and small groups.

3. When underwriters project the claims of small groups, which of these are a major consideration?
   I.   The average level of claims of groups of the same size.
   II. The general characteristics of the group.
   III. The claims experience of the group.

   a. I and II only.

   b. I and III only.

   c. II and III only.

   d. I, II, and III.

4. Guaranteed issue means that insurers must usually offer coverage to

    a. employer-sponsored groups.

    b. government-sponsored groups.

    c. large groups.

    d. small groups.

5. An insurer normally declines to insure a group formed solely for the purpose of purchasing insurance mainly because the group would

    a. be subject to adverse selection.

    b. have a low rate of participation.

    c. not have the ability to properly administer itself.

    d. not exist for very long.

6. Compared to women, men have

    a. higher health insurance claims overall, but lower disability claims.

    b. lower health insurance claims overall, but higher disability claims.

    c. higher overall health insurance claims and higher disability claims.

    d. lower overall health insurance claims and lower disability claims.

Answers

1. The process of deciding whether and on what terms to offer coverage.

2. The benefits that the insurer will provide, the premiums that the policyholder will pay, and other provisions of the contract.

3. Almost always.

4. The terms of coverage to be offered.

5. The underwriter must write a policy with terms such that the insurer will earn enough money from premiums to pay claims and still make a profit; to do this, the underwriter must know at least roughly what the level of claims will be.

6. How much the insurer must charge in premiums in order to earn enough to cover claims and make a profit, and what benefit provisions must be written into the policy to ensure that claims do not go above the predicted level.

7. Underwriters look at the average experience of groups in the past and assume that future experience will be similar.

8. The underwriter assumes that the level of claims of the group she is considering will be similar to the level of claims of other groups with the same general characteristics (such as the same average age).

9. Already have insurance but want to change insurers.

10. The underwriter assumes that the group's past experience will be repeated in the future.

11. A number of people have the option of receiving and paying for coverage. A larger proportion of those who are more likely to become ill choose coverage, and a smaller proportion of those less likely to become ill choose not to have coverage.

12. If adverse selection occurs, the covered group is not truly average, but rather has a higher level of claims than an average group. Consequently, the claims of the group may be higher than the underwriter predicted.

13. The underwriter must strive to offer terms that are attractive to the prospect, so that the prospect will choose the insurer's offer over another.

14. In underwriting manuals.

15. Issued by each insurer for its own use.

16. Regulations do not usually allow the insurer to decline to offer coverage to such groups.

17. Such groups are almost always acceptable risks.

18. He cannot predict the number and amounts of claims that a group will make without first making assumptions about what kind of claims group members will have the right to make.

19. The benefits requested by the group (perhaps modified to reflect the benefits that the new insurer is willing to provide).

20. A continuation of existing benefits, modified to take into account any changes in benefits requested by the group, as well as the benefits that the new insurer is willing to provide.

21. He must ascertain the characteristics of the group (average age, gender distribution, etc.) and apply this information to statistical knowledge.

22. In the underwriting manual.

23. He must determine the credibility of the information and use it to accurately predict future claims.

24. • He must carefully examine all information to determine if the group diverges from the norm in any way that would warrant making an exception to the insurer's standard procedures. This includes probing for any indications of adverse selection.

   • He must calculate expenses not related to claims, such as the administrative costs of providing coverage.

25. Either or both.

26. In the rating manual.

27. Subject to state laws and regulations.

28. The benefit provisions requested by the group resulted in high claims projections and consequently unacceptably high premium rates.

29. They analyze the claims and other expenses of the policy to determine whether modifications in terms should be made and what they should be.

30. They do studies to determine the impact of the suggested changes.

31. 50.

32. • Other things being equal, actual experience is a better predictor than statistical averages.

   • The larger the body of data that the prediction is based on, the more accurate the prediction will be.

33. The actual claims experience of the group may be useful, but because it is such a small statistical sample, it may not be as accurate a predictor as the average experience of many other groups.

34. The group has enough members to make a statistically reliable sample, and so the actual claims experience of the group will predict more accurately than statistical studies.

35. Is usually roughly the same every year.

36. Fluctuates greatly from year to year.

37. Because its level of claims is usually roughly the same every year.

38. Because its level of claims fluctuates greatly from year to year.

39. Because claims projections for large groups are based on data that is both specific to the group in question and large enough to be statistically reliable, while projections for small groups are based largely on general averages.

40. Many small groups are combined (for statistical purposes only) into one large group, and claims projections are made for that group. This allows underwriters to base claims projections on a large body of actual claims experience, just as they do in underwriting large groups.

41. The fact that claims projections for small groups are less accurate than for large groups.

42. An inaccurate claims projection for a large

group has a much greater impact on an insurer's overall finances.

43. Averages.

44. Actual claims experience of the group.

45. Both.

46. Reduce the group's rates or give an experience refund if a provision for this is included in the contract.

47. Because one individual can have an important impact on claims levels.

48. They limit the use of preexisting condition exclusions and prohibit insurers from excluding individual employees from coverage based on their health status.

49. Insurers serving the small group market must accept any small group that applies and that is eligible under the law.

50. HIPAA and the small group market reforms enacted by many states in the early 1990s.

51. Does not include.

52. Small groups.

53. They keep plans for small groups simple and limit benefit variations.

54. Rarely.

55. • The group has low participation.

• The group is fictitious.

• The underwriter believes the policyholder is not able to adequately administer the plan.

• The underwriter believes the group will not stay with the insurer for a reasonable period of time.

56. The enrolled group is likely to have a much larger than average number of individuals with health problems. In other words, adverse selection is likely to occur.

57. A group created solely for the purpose of obtaining insurance for its members.

58. Underwriting is based on the assumption that any group being considered is a random sample of people and that therefore the group includes an average mix of healthy and less healthy individuals. For groups that form for a reason other than insurance (such as employment), this is very likely the case. On the other hand, a group formed to obtain

insurance for its members is almost certainly made up of people who are very likely to incur medical expenses. This is another example of adverse selection.

59. So that the insurer can recover its acquisition expenses.

60. The expenses an insurer incurs when it first insures a group.

61. The costs of sales activities, underwriting, and contract issuance.

62. Temporary businesses (such as those created for a specific limited project) or businesses in financial difficulties.

63. Age, gender, dependent participation, occupation or type of business, income, and geographical location.

64. Claims projections for most large groups are based on the actual claims experience of the group, which already reflects the impact of these characteristics.

65. Older.

66. The average age of the group.

67. Women.

68. Women.

69. Men.

70. The proportion of men and women in the group.

71. Dependents are children and spouses, and age and gender affect claims.

72. The increase in single-parent households, the decrease in the average number of children per family, and the increase in working women.

73. Dependent participation is usually low if employees' spouses have coverage from their own employers.

74. State workers' compensation programs.

75. Are covered.

76. They do.

77. These businesses pay low wages and so tend to attract workers who cannot meet the health standards of more selective employers.

78. Because people with higher-than-average incomes generally get more frequent and higher-priced medical care.

79. Because low-paying jobs are more likely to involve working conditions that indirectly cause health problems.

80. The cost of claims only.

81. Urban areas.

82. The business may hire very few new employees because of financial difficulties.

83. The business may have high turnover.

84. High administrative costs; a rapid and significant change in the characteristics of the group, possibly making rates inadequate.

85. Experience.

86. Averages.

87. To look for any indications of problems.

88. To get a better rate, better service, or more managed care options.

89. The group may be seeking a change because its present insurer has or is about to raise rates as a result of very high claims.

90. Examining the data to determine that they are complete, accurate, and reliable.

91. How accurately the data will predict future claims.

92. The size of the group and the length of time covered by the data.

93. Is roughly the same every year, but has significant fluctuations.

94. More.

95. Will likely continue.

96. May or may not continue.

97. An unusual accident. Or a catastrophic illness the victim of which has died.

98. A chronic condition that will continue indefinitely.

99. May disregard part of the claim.

100. Must include all of the claim.

101. Claims projections and premium rates for large groups are generally based solely on such data; also, the larger the group, the greater the financial impact on the insurer of an inaccurate projection of claims.

102. It involves the examination and analysis of claims data.

103. He must make decisions based on his own experience.

104. Usually either.

105. The present insurer may have proposed, as a condition of renewal, changes such as increased deductibles or additional limitations that were intended to solve specific claim problems.

106. Study these provisions to determine what impact they may have, decide whether to include them in the new plan, and notify the policyholder of any changes.

107. May be covered under different plans.

108. Some classes may be provided with coverage and not others.

109. It creates a larger group.

110. The hourly workers' health plan may be determined by collective bargaining between the employer and a union.

111. That it be sufficiently large.

112. Executives may request plan provisions with the intention of ensuring coverage for a specific health condition of one of the executives or a member of an executive's family.

113. These employees have high turnover and consequently high administrative costs.

114. A contract provision that requires, when employees have the option of enrolling in a coverage or not, that a minimum number or percentage of all employees enroll.

115. If only a small percentage of employees enroll, the enrolled group will have a larger than average number of individuals with health problems. Minimum enrollment requirements do not allow such a small percentage of enrollment.

116. 75 percent.

117. Exclude dependents with other coverage in determining if the requirement for dependent participation has been met.

118. When only a few employees choose dependent coverage.

119. The employee.

120. The employee. (The employer may also pay a part, but it is the employee's contribution that makes it contributory.)

121. Noncontributory.

122. Since all employees participate, a larger group is created, there is no possibility of adverse selection, and administration is simplified.

123. Employees do not choose to participate or not.

124. In contributory plans employees must enroll individually, and in some plans late entrants must submit evidence of insurability. In noncontributory plans all employees are automatically enrolled.

125. The employee.

126. a. The insurer may not be able to offer a fully adequate plan, since the average employee may not be able to pay the full cost of such a plan.

    b. Due to the high cost to employees, participation may be low, meaning that the group may be small and adverse selection a potential problem.

    c. Since any increases in premium rates will be passed on in full to the employee, maintaining participation will be difficult.

    d. An employer's refusal to contribute financially may indicate a lack of interest in the plan that could result in poor administration and a lack of cooperation with the insurer.

127. Most insurers only offer such coverages as long-term care insurance or voluntary accidental death and dismemberment insurance on a fully contributory basis. Even then, they usually insist on minimum participation requirements.

128. Some.

129. Some benefit provisions might have resulted in high claims. The underwriter will have to require modifications of these provisions or a premium rate sufficient to cover them.

130. If the group is large enough to warrant special plan design, if the proposed premium rates are high enough to pay for the additional benefits, and if the insurer is able to administratively handle the benefits.

131. Either.

132. They can indicate policyholder financial problems. Also, if the benefits of a plan are inadequate, many employees will seek additional coverage by purchasing individual policies, which may result in overinsurance.

133. Group policies only.

134. The contribution required from the employee is often large, and this can lead to low participation, a small group, and possibly adverse selection. Low-income employees will be especially likely to choose not to participate, giving the group a high average income.

135. The choice of generous benefits may be motivated by the desire to provide broad coverage for an existing condition of a key employee.

136. It expects that the division of responsibilities between the policyholder and insurer will remain roughly the same, that procedures will remain the same, and that existing records will be carried over.

137. She must determine what the expectations of the policyholder are; determine if these expectations conflict with the standard operations and procedures of the new insurer; decide if the insurer will be able to meet these expectations or if modifications will have to be made; determine the cost of any special administrative provisions made to accommodate the policyholder and adjust premiums accordingly; and notify the policyholder of any changes.

138. • Will the new insurer's standard billing and claims procedures be acceptable to the policyholder?

    • Will the policyholder accept self-billing?

    • Will separate record keeping, billing, and claim processing be required for separate locations?

139. An arrangement whereby the policyholder takes responsibility for the billing of individual members.

140. That no group member lose benefit

payments for an existing health condition when the group's plan is transferred. They also usually prohibit the new insurer from applying preexisting condition limitations to individuals who are already members of the existing plan.

141. State. Group only.

142. HIPAA.

143. Some group insurance policies stipulate that if insureds are receiving benefits for some conditions (such as total disability) when the contract is terminated, they will continue to receive benefits for some period of time after termination.

144. So that the new insurer does not provide duplicate benefits.

145. The insurer determines what the renewal rate would be for one of its current groups with the same claims experience and the same benefits.

146. By using standard rates from rating manuals.

147. Both employers and insurers.

148. More complex.

149. She must estimate savings in claims and adjust premiums accordingly.

150. • The proportion of plan members who participate in managed care;

   • the portion of claims attributable to the managed care options of the plan;

   • trends in the above two areas;

   • the discounts and savings attributable to managed care under the existing HMO and/or PPO; and

   • the discounts and savings projected under the new HMO and/or PPO.

151. Employee data, the group's claim history, the employer's prior insurance history, and the plan provisions desired or required by the group.

152. The number of employees participating, the number eligible, and whether there are any excluded classes.

153. It helps the underwriter determine whether the employer is likely to continue with the insurer.

154. Age, gender, earnings, dependents, and occupation.

155. Small.

156. They visit the employer's business, report on any adverse working conditions, help verify the eligibility information supplied by the employer in the RFP, and submit an inspection report to the insurer.

157. Employers are required to distribute annual health plan experience reports to their employees and to file similar information with the U.S. Department of Labor. Underwriters can use this information.

158. Large (100 or more insured employees).

159. Agents, brokers, and group representatives.

160. Premiums will be too high and the company will lose business to competitors.

161. Premiums will not be sufficient to meet costs and the company will lose money.

Answers to Practice Exam Questions

1. c

2. c

3. a

4. d

5. a

6. d

16 UNDERWRITING OF INDIVIDUAL HEALTH INSURANCE

Introduction (Page 143)

1. How is underwriting of individual health insurance similar to group underwriting?

2. What are the three main differences between individual and group underwriting?

Principles of Individual Underwriting (Pages 143–144)

3. In (group / individual / both group and individual) underwriting, it is usually assumed that, barring special circumstances, an offer of coverage will be made.

4. Why is the prediction of claims essential to underwriting for both groups and individuals?

5. How are claims projected for an individual?

6. How are general characteristics used in projecting claims for individuals?

7. What activity do individual underwriters engage in that group underwriters do not?

8. Why do individual underwriters not accept all applicants on the assumption that the claims of the more healthy and the less healthy people they insure will balance out?

9. How does a preexisting group (such as all the employees of a business) differ from a random group of people seeking individual insurance?

10. What actions can an underwriter take if an applicant for individual insurance is likely to have a high level of claims?

11. Insurers are (always / usually / never) allowed to decline to offer coverage to an individual.

12. What restrictions does HIPAA place on an insurer's right to decline to offer coverage to an individual?

13. Some state laws (require guaranteed availability of individual insurance / limit rate differentials to different applicants / either or both).

Adjusting for General Characteristics (Pages 144–145)

14. In individual underwriting, general characteristics such as age and gender are used (quite differently / in largely the same way) as in group underwriting.

15. Which general characteristics are particularly important in underwriting individual disability income and accidental death and dismemberment policies?

16. Persons in professional occupations and those with high incomes have (fewer / more) disability claims and (shorter / longer) periods of disability than average.

17. Persons in occupations that require heavy manual labor or where there are accidental hazards have (fewer / more) disability claims and (shorter / longer) periods of disability than average.

18. For individual disability income insurance, insurers have established classes of occupations. What are these classes based on?

19. How do insurers use these classes?

20. Lower premiums, more liberal benefits, and higher maximum benefits are available to the classes with (lower / higher) claims.

21. In underwriting individual medical expense insurance, occupation (is / is not) a major factor, and premiums usually (vary / do not vary) by occupation.

22. Thomas is a sky-diving instructor, which is considered an extremely hazardous occupation. He applies to Big State Insurance for individual medical expense insurance. What actions might Big State take?

Analyzing Information on the Individual (Pages 145–146)

23. What are the two most important factors in determining the probability of an individual having future medical problems?

24. In assessing an individual's current physical condition and medical history, what two questions must an individual underwriter ask?

25. In what ways can an individual's current medical condition and medical history affect his future level of claims?

26. What is an example of how one medical condition could lead to another condition?

27. A (majority / minority) of medical conditions recur or have latent complications that do not emerge until much later.

28. Most previous medical problems can be disregarded provided certain conditions are met. What are these conditions?

29. Why is an applicant's financial situation an important consideration in underwriting individual disability income policies?

30. Why must disability income not be higher than or nearly equal to an insured's regular income?

31. Marie has a high net worth, but her assets are not producing substantial investment income. Why would an underwriter considering her for an individual disability income policy take her net worth into account?

The Individual Underwriting Process (Pages 146–152)

32. What is the main source of information for individual underwriting?

33. In the application, the applicant supplies general information and makes statements about what?

34. The (applicant / agent) usually fills out the application.

35. How do applications differ?

36. What information is typically provided by the agent on the back of the application?

37. The underwriting of an applicant is based on (the application and the agent's statements only / the application, the agent' statements, and additional information / either).

38. If, in addition to the application and the agent's statements, the underwriter wants to seek information from outside sources, what must she have?

39. Most insurers require more frequent use of medical examinations and physicians' statements for older applicants. Why?

40. What information is provided in a medical examination?

41. The information on a medical examination form is provided by (the examining physician / the applicant / both).

42. The medical examination form is signed by (the examining physician / the applicant / both).

43. A person who is uninsurable because of his previous medical history (might / will not) pass a medical examination.

◆ 44. Who conducts a **paramedical examination?**

45. What information is provided in a paramedical examination?

46. What are the advantages of a paramedical examination over a medical examination?

◆ 47. Who provides the information in an **attending physician statement (APS)?**

48. What information is provided in the APS?

49. When is an APS requested?

50. The most complete source of information on medical history is (the application / the medical examination / the attending physician statement).

51. Laboratory tests are (a routine part of a medical or paramedical examination / requested by the underwriter as a follow-up to an examination or APS / either).

52. Why are blood tests particularly useful?

53. What is some of the information revealed by blood tests?

54. What laboratory test reveals tobacco use?

55. Which test provides information on heart disease?

◆ 56. What do **inspection companies** do?

57. What information is included in an inspection report?

58. How do inspection companies and insurers deal with privacy issues?

59. Income documentation is generally necessary for (medical expense insurance / disability income insurance).

60. How do applicants usually document their income?

61. What role does MIB, Inc. play in underwriting?

62. What is the corporate status of MIB?

◆ 63. What is an **impairment**?

64. What is an example of a nonmedical impairment?

65. Joan is applying for coverage with Epsilon Insurance, a member company of MIB. What are Epsilon's responsibilities to MIB?

66. Joan later applies for coverage at Omega Insurance, also a member of MIB. What can underwriters at Omega do?

67. Omega will be able to obtain information on (the type and amount of insurance Joan applied for / whether Epsilon issued coverage to Joan / both / neither).

68. Which of the following does MIB do? (Records information reported by member companies / employs investigators / obtains copies of records from agents, doctors, or hospitals).

69. What is the primary usefulness of information from MIB?

70. What is the Disability Income Record System (DIRS)?

71. Member companies report to DIRS (that someone has applied for an individual disability income policy / any medical information discovered in underwriting / both).

72. If an application to a member company meets minimums in two areas, the company must report the application to DIRS. What are these areas?

73. What is the main usefulness of the DIRS information exchange?

74. Why are some health insurance companies not members of MIB?

75. What does an MIB associate membership for disability income insurance provide to insurers?

76. Individuals (have / do not have) the right to challenge the accuracy of any information reported to MIB.

Individual Underwriters and Sales Personnel (Page 152)

77. How can individual underwriters support the field sales force?

Practice Exam Questions

1. Insurers usually have the legal right to decline to offer coverage to
   I.   individuals.
   II. small groups.
   III. large groups.

   a. I and II only.

   b. I and III only.

   c. II and II only.

   d. I, II, and III.

2. People in professional jobs and those with high incomes have

   a. fewer disability claims and shorter periods of disability than average.

   b. fewer disability claims but longer periods of disability than average.

   c. more disability claims and longer periods of disability than average.

   d. more disability claims but shorter periods of disability than average.

3. Which is the most complete source of information on an applicant's medical history?

   a. Application.

   b. Attending physician's statement.

   c. Medical examination.

   d. Paramedical examination.

4. Which laboratory test is considered the most useful because it gives information on a wide range of conditions at a reasonable cost?

   a. Blood test.

   b. Electrocardiogram.

   c. Urinalysis.

   d. Vital capacity test.

Answers

1. They are both based on the same principles and involve many of the same activities.

2. • Individual underwriters often decline to offer coverage, while group underwriters rarely do.

   • Individual underwriters concern themselves with both averages and the health, occupation, and financial status of individuals, while group underwriters rely only on group averages.

   • Individual and group underwriters use different sources of information.

3. Group only.

4. In both cases the underwriter must ensure that the level of claims will not be higher than the premiums received.

5. By relying on the average experience of many individuals.

6. Projections for the person being underwritten are based on averages of people with the same general characteristics (age, gender, etc.).

7. They examine each individual to determine whether for some reason (such as an existing medical condition) she is significantly more likely than the average person to make claims.

8. Because of the potential for adverse selection.

9. In a preexisting group, there is usually an average mix of people who are more healthy and people who are less healthy. A random group of people seeking individual coverage has a disproportionately large number of people with medical problems or a high likelihood of becoming ill.

10. She can decline to provide coverage, provide modified coverage, or adjust premiums.

11. Usually.

12. HIPAA guarantees the availability of individual health insurance coverage without preexisting condition limitations to certain individuals who have lost group health coverage.

13. Either or both.

14. In largely the same way.

15. Occupation and income.

16. Fewer, shorter.

17. More, longer.

18. Levels of claims.

19. To determine premium rates and the type and amount of coverage offered.

20. Lower.

21. Is not; do not vary.

22. It may refuse to issue coverage, or it may issue a policy that excludes occupational injuries.

23. The individual's current physical condition and his medical history.

24. • Does the applicant's health history and current physical condition differ significantly from the average?

    • What is the probable impact of current medical conditions and previous medical history on future claims?

25. He may currently have a condition that will result in claims (possibly even leading to hospitalization or disability), or that could lead to an additional illness or injury, or that could prolong a disability from an unrelated cause. He may also have had a condition in the past that could recur or lead to complications.

26. Epilepsy increases the chances of an injury; obesity can lead to cardiovascular problems.

27. A minority.

28. Recovery has been prompt, and there is no evidence of any residual impairment.

29. Benefits must be at such a level that the insured's disability income is not a great deal less than her pre-disability income, but not so high that disability income is greater than or almost the same as pre-disability income.

30. Because the insured would have no incentive to return to work.

31. If she became disabled, Marie could shift her assets to income-generating investments, and this revenue combined with her disability benefits could give her an income close to or greater than her pre-disability income.

32. The application.

33. His current physical condition and medical history.

34. The agent (based on the applicant's answers to questions).

35. Some applications are used for only one type of insurance while others are used for a variety of coverages.

36. • How long and how well the agent has known the applicant;

    • the applicant's approximate net worth, annual earned income, and income from sources other than employment;

    • clarification of any information on the application that is questionable or unclear;

    • any special circumstances or special problems not otherwise noted on the application; and

    • any other information the agent has regarding the applicant that is not included on the application but that might be relevant to underwriting.

37. Either. (The underwriter may or may not seek information in addition to the application and the agent's statements.)

38. The applicant's signed authorization form.

39. Older people are more likely to have medical problems than younger people and are more likely to have problems not specifically asked about in the application.

40. Height and weight, pulse, blood pressure, and other findings.

41. Both. (The applicant fills out the nonmedical sections.)

42. Both.

43. Might.

44. A medical technician (under the supervision of a physician).

45. Medical history, height, weight, pulse rate, blood pressure, and urinalysis results.

46. Paramedical examinations are more economical, they can be easier and more convenient for the applicant, and they free physicians from conducting insurance examinations.

47. The applicant's regular physician.

48. Details of the applicant's current health and

medical history, including exactly what the applicant has been treated for, the dates and duration of treatment, whether there was a complete recovery, and the involvement of any consulting physicians.

49. When the application or medical examination discloses a serious medical condition or questionable history.

50. The attending physician statement.

51. Either.

52. They provide information on a wide range of conditions for a reasonable cost.

53. Elevated cholesterol and lipids, liver abnormalities, drug use, diabetes, disorders of the kidneys, and the presence of the human immunodeficiency virus (HIV).

54. Urinalysis.

55. Electrocardiogram.

56. They investigate applicants and submit a written inspection report to the underwriter.

57. The applicant's occupation, financial status, and health history.

58. They have established procedures for keeping information confidential.

59. Disability income insurance.

60. They certify their annual income in the application or an attachment and may also have to submit a copy of their latest income tax return.

61. It manages an information exchange that member companies can use to obtain information about applicants for coverage.

62. It is an association of life and health insurance companies.

63. A condition or circumstance that might make a person a bad insurance risk.

64. A bad driving record.

65. If, during underwriting, Epsilon discovers that Joan has one of the impairments on MIB's list of impairments, Epsilon must report this fact to MIB.

66. Check MIB's database to see if Joan has any impairment that was discovered by Epsilon but not revealed by Joan.

67. Neither. (Companies report to MIB only the existence of an impairment.)

68. MIB only records information reported by member companies.

69. It alerts underwriters that a problem may exist and that further investigation is necessary.

70. An information exchange for disability income insurance maintained by MIB.

71. Only that someone has applied.

72. Amount of monthly benefit and length of benefit period.

73. It helps member companies find out if a person is overinsuring himself by getting coverage from more than one company.

74. To qualify for full membership in MIB an insurance company must have a medical director and sell life insurance.

75. DIRS services and MIB information for a disability application.

76. Have.

77. By maintaining close communication with agents, providing them with information about the status of pending applications, and processing applications in a timely fashion.

Answers to Practice Exam Questions

1. b

2. a

3. b

4. a

17 REINSURANCE AND REINSURERS

Introduction (Page 155)

✦ 1. What is **reinsurance**?

How Reinsurance Works (Pages 155–156)

2. Matterhorn Insurance sells a comprehensive major medical policy to John. Matterhorn purchases reinsurance on this policy from Gibraltar Insurance. If John suffers a loss and Matterhorn has to pay claims, what will be the responsibility of Gibraltar?

3. Suppose John's policy had an overall maximum benefit of $2,000,000, and suppose that Matterhorn arranged for Gibraltar to accept the second million dollars of that risk. If John suffers a catastrophic illness and makes claims totaling $1,300,000, how much of these claims will Gibraltar reimburse Matterhorn for?

✦ 4. In reinsurance, which company is the **direct-writing insurer** or the **ceding insurer**?

✦ 5. In reinsurance, which company is the **reinsurer**?

6. Why is the insurer that issues the original policy known as the direct-writing insurer?

7. Why is the insurer that issues the original policy known also as the ceding insurer?

8. In the above example, (Gibraltar / Matterhorn) is the direct-writing or ceding insurer.

9. In the above example, (Gibraltar / Matterhorn) is the reinsurer.

10. A contract exists between the policyholder and (the direct-writing insurer only / the direct-writing insurer and the reinsurer).

11. Reinsurance (relieves / does not relieve) the direct-writing insurer of part of its obligation to pay benefits to the policyholder.

12. When a reinsurer is responsible for a loss, the reinsurer (pays the policyholder / reimburses the direct-writing insurer, which pays the policyholder).

✦ 13. How does **retrocession** work?

14. Retrocession generally occurs if the amount of reinsurance is (small / large).

15. Why does a reinsurer retrocede?

The Advantages of Reinsurance (Page 156)

16. Reinsurance transfers risk from the (ceding insurer to the reinsurer / reinsurer to the ceding insurer).

17. Reinsurance or no reinsurance?

    a. An insurer assumes the risk of having to pay a very large amount in claims at one time.

    b. An insurer avoids this risk by paying premiums to another insurer.

18. What four advantages does reinsurance give insurers?

19. Why is it important for insurers to avoid fluctuations in their profit/loss balance from year to year?

Types of Reinsurance (Page 157)

20. Matterhorn Insurance and Gibraltar Insurance make an agreement whereby Matterhorn must cede any risk over $500,000 to Gibraltar and Gibraltar must accept it. This is an example of (**automatic** / **facultative**) reinsurance.

21. Treasury Insurance often uses Gibraltar Insurance as a reinsurer, but the companies have no formal agreement. Treasury simply asks Gibraltar to reinsure some risks and Gibraltar sometimes accepts and sometimes refuses. This is an example of (**automatic** / **facultative**) reinsurance.

22. What is a reinsurance agreement called?

Technical Assistance Provided by Reinsurers (Page 157)

23. In what areas do reinsurers provide insurers with technical assistance?

24. What kinds of underwriting support do reinsurers provide?

25. What types of insurers particularly need a reinsurer's technical assistance?

The Health Reinsurance Field (Pages 157–158)

26. Why is health reinsurance a more recent development than life reinsurance?

27. There are more (life reinsurers / health reinsurers).

Practice Exam Questions

1. John purchases an insurance policy from Rocky Mountain Insurance. Rocky Mountain purchases reinsurance on this policy from Appalachian Insurance. Appalachian in turn purchases reinsurance on its part of the policy from Ozark Insurance. Appalachian's transaction with Ozark is an example of

    a. automatic reinsurance.

    b. facultative reinsurance.

    c. normal reinsurance.

    d. retrocession.

2. Which of these is a disadvantage of reinsurance?

    a. A reduction in the ability to experiment with new coverages.

    b. Large fluctuations in profit/loss balance from year to year.

    c. The expense of reinsurance premiums.

    d. The possibility of very large unexpected claim losses.

Answers

1. An arrangement whereby an insurance company uses another insurance company to manage and share risk.

2. Gibraltar may have to reimburse Matterhorn for part of the claims Matterhorn paid John. (Whether Gibraltar actually has to reimburse Matterhorn in a given situation will depend on the exact terms of their agreement.)

3. $300,000.

4. The company that issues the original policy.

5. The company that agrees to accept part of the risk from the direct-writing insurer.

6. Because it writes, or issues, the coverage directly to the policyholder.

7. Because it cedes, or passes on, part of the risk to the other insurer.

8. Matterhorn.

9. Gibraltar.

10. The direct-writing insurer only.

11. Does not relieve. The contract between the policyholder and the direct-writing insurer and the obligations of the direct-writing insurer are unaffected by reinsurance.

12. Reimburses the direct-writing insurer.

13. A reinsurer passes a portion of the risk it assumes in reinsurance to another reinsurer.

14. Large.

15. To share and manage risk.

16. Ceding insurer to the reinsurer.

17. a. No reinsurance.

    b. Reinsurance.

18. • Protection from very large unexpected claim losses;

    • avoidance of wide fluctuations in their profit/loss balance from year to year;

    • the ability to accept business that presents a large risk; and

    • the ability to experiment with new coverages.

19. So they can plan and grow in an orderly way.

20. Automatic.

21. Facultative.

22. A treaty.

23. Claims, administration, technology, actuarial science, product development, market analysis, and underwriting.

24. Classifying occupations, underwriting difficult cases, recommending whether changing medical and nonmedical requirements is feasible, training for underwriters, and supplying underwriting manuals.

25. Small insurers and insurers new to the field.

26. Reinsurance is most needed when the maximum amounts that insurers might have to pay on policies are high, and before the 1960s these amounts were fairly low for health insurance.

27. Life reinsurers.

Answers to Practice Exam Questions

1. d
2. c

18 HEALTH INSURANCE PAST, PRESENT, AND FUTURE

The 19th and Early 20th Centuries: The Emergence of Modern Health Insurance Coverages and the Beginnings of the Health Insurance Industry (Pages 160–162)

1. People have made arrangements to avoid financial loss because of an accident or illness for centuries. Why then do we say that modern health insurance began in the 19th century?

2. One of the earliest modern health insurance coverages was (medical expense insurance / disability income insurance / accident insurance).

3. The first accident insurance paid benefits in the form of (monthly payments / reimbursement for expenses / a lump sum).

4. How did **sickness insurance** differ from modern medical expense insurance?

5. How was sickness insurance similar to modern disability income insurance?

6. Why was the coverage offered by early sickness insurance limited?

7. Group insurance began (about the same time as / much later than) individual insurance.

8. How did intense competition cause many early health insurance companies to fail?

9. How did the inadequacy of underwriting information cause many early health insurance companies to fail?

10. What aspect of early health insurance policies damaged the credibility of the industry?

11. Why were there few cooperative efforts among early insurers to solve the problems of the industry?

12. In the early 20th century, the Armstrong Investigation examined insurance companies. What was the result?

13. What kinds of actions did many states take in the period following the Armstrong Investigation?

14. What was the purpose of the Standard Provisions Law?

The Great Depression, World War II, and the Growth of Employment-Based Health Insurance (Pages 162–164)

15. Why did the Great Depression of the 1930s have such a devastating effect on the health insurance industry?

16. What were four positive developments of the Depression period?

17. What was the first form of medical expense insurance?

18. Hospital expense insurance covered (hospital services only / surgeons' and physicians' services / both).

19. The first hospital expense insurance was offered by (insurers / hospitals).

20. What is the historical significance of the plan sponsored by Baylor University Hospital in Dallas, Texas in the late 1920s?

21. What was the origin of the Blue Cross plans?

22. In the 1930s, group hospital expense insurance was provided by (hospitals / employers and commercial insurers / both).

23. What coverages were created to fill the gaps of hospital expense insurance?

24. What was the origin of the Blue Shield surgical-medical plans?

25. How did each of these developments encourage the spread of employer-sponsored group health insurance in the 1930s and 1940s?

    a. Government anti-inflation efforts during World War II.

    b. The growth of labor unions.

    c. Federal tax policy.

26. What important ruling concerning health insurance was made by the National Labor Relations Board and confirmed by the Supreme Court in the late 1940s?

The 1950s and 1960s: The Modern Health Insurance Environment Takes Shape (Pages 164–166)

27. What were the three main features of the health insurance environment that emerged after World War II?

28. What is the principle feature that distinguishes the health care environment of today from that of the 1950s and 1960s?

29. What was the most important new product developed in the post-World-War-II era?

30. What were some of the other products introduced during this period?

31. The Uniform Policy Provisions Law (UPPL) was adopted at least in essence by (some / most / all) states.

32. Congress passed the McCarran-Ferguson Act in the late 1940s. What was the purpose of this act?

33. The Medicare and Medicaid programs began in the (1950s / 1960s / 1970s).

Recent and Current Trends (Pages 167–172)

34. What are some of the changes in family structure and the work force that have occurred since the 1950s?

35. How have insurers responded to these changes?

36. Why is the average age of the population rising?

37. How have group insurance plans changed in response to the aging of the population?

◆ 38. What is **consumerism**?

39. What are some of the results of the consumer movement in these areas of insurance?

    a. New coverages.

    b. State laws.

    c. Federal legislation.

40. What are some of the causes for the increased utilization of medical services that has occurred in recent decades?

41. The increased utilization of health care and the higher cost of that care have led to higher health insurance claims and higher premiums for consumers. What are four of the ways insurers have responded to this problem?

42. Which of these responses has had the greatest impact?

43. In what two ways has the shift to managed care occurred?

44. How does requiring insureds to pay greater amounts in deductibles and coinsurance address the problem of high premiums?

45. What are the changes in each of these areas that have contributed to the recent rise in the number of uninsured people?

    a. Employment.

    b. Health care.

    c. Laws.

    d. Medicaid.

46. Which of these changes has had the most impact?

47. How has the increasing cost of health care led to more uninsureds?

48. How have mandated benefits contributed to the growth in uninsureds?

49. What are four results of the highly competitive environment that has developed in the health insurance industry in recent years?

50. What are three ways in which mergers and acquisitions make companies more competitive?

51. Because of their competitive disadvantage, much of the recent merger and acquisition activity has been among (stock companies / mutual companies).

52. In what three ways has the shift to managed care been a factor in the increase in mergers and acquisitions?

♦ 53. How does a **joint venture** work?

54. What are three of the new types of joint ventures?

♦ 55. How does **private labeling** work?

56. For what kinds of products is private labeling most common?

Practice Exam Questions

1. Which of these coverages was developed first?

    a. Accident insurance.

    b. Group insurance.

    c. Major medical insurance.

    d. Medical expense insurance.

2. The health insurance environment that emerged in the 1950s and 1960s was very much like today's environment. What was the main difference?

    a. Employment-based group plans were not yet dominant.

    b. Managed care was not very important.

    c. The role of government was not very important.

    d. There were not very many kinds of coverage offered.

3. Which of these developments has been the most important cause of the increase in the number of people without health insurance?

    a. Laws mandating that certain coverages include certain benefits.

    b. The erosion of Medicaid coverage for the poor.

    c. The increase in part-time, temporary, and service sector employment.

    d. The rising cost of health care.

4. **What approach taken by insurers to contain the cost of health insurance has had the greatest impact?**

   a. Controlling company expenses.

   b. Improving company efficiency.

   c. Improving underwriting.

   d. Shifting to managed care.

Answers

1. Before the 19ᵗʰ century there were simple forms of insurance providing some protection, but modern coverages and techniques did not begin until that time.

2. Accident insurance.

3. A lump sum.

4. Sickness insurance paid a pre-set amount (or a pre-set amount per day), whereas medical expense insurance reimburses the insured for the actual medical expenses she incurs.

5. It paid a pre-set amount, which was used in part to compensate for lost income due to inability to work.

6. Companies had few reliable statistics on the frequency of illnesses, making prediction of claims difficult, so they tried to avoid the risk of paying a very large amount in claims by restricting coverages.

7. Much later. (The first policy was issued in the early 20th century.)

8. In order to compete, many companies cut their premium rates so low that they could not make a profit.

9. Insurers could not reliably predict claims, so they often set premiums rates that were insufficient to cover claims. Also, many companies accepted bad risks.

10. Some companies tried to reduce their risk by issuing policies with many restrictions, some of which were hidden in the fine print.

11. Because of the environment of intense competition.

12. State regulation of insurance, which had

begun in a limited way in the 19ᵗʰ century, was expanded and tightened.

13. They enacted laws dictating the provisions of insurance policies and governing the operations of insurers, and they implemented closer supervision of the industry to ensure compliance with statutes and regulations.

14. To make the operating provisions of health insurance contracts more uniform.

15. People had little money to pay for "extras" like insurance, and many people falsely claimed sickness disability benefits in order to have some source of income.

16. • Companies became more financially cautious.

    • There was greater cooperation among companies.

    • Medical expense insurance developed and spread.

    • Employment-based group health insurance emerged.

17. Hospital expense insurance.

18. Hospital services only.

19. Hospitals.

20. It was the first group hospital expense insurance policy.

21. Around the country several hospitals in the same state or part of a state banded together to offer group hospital expense insurance.

22. Both.

23. Surgical expense insurance (to cover surgeons' fees) and medical expense insurance (to cover physicians' charges).

24. In the 1930s the state medical society in California established the California Physicians' Service.

25. a. Employers were not allowed to raise salaries to attract and retain workers, but they could provide fringe benefits, including group health insurance.

    b. As unions gained power, they began to demand that employers provide group health insurance plans.

    c. Employers were allowed to deduct as a business expense their expenditures for employee health coverage, and individuals did not have to pay income tax on employment-based health coverage.

26. That unions had a right to demand group health insurance as part of collective bargaining.

27. • Most people got their health insurance through an employment-based group plan.

    • A wide variety of coverages was available.

    • Government had a role as a regulator and in providing for certain populations.

28. The current importance of managed care.

29. Major medical coverage.

30. Comprehensive major medical insurance, dental expense insurance, credit health insurance, long-term disability income insurance, vision care benefits, extended care facility benefits, prescription drug benefits, and group plans for trade associations, professional associations, and multiple-employer trusts.

31. All.

32. The Supreme Court ruled that because insurance is interstate commerce, the federal government has the right to regulate it, but in the McCarran-Ferguson Act Congress granted this right largely to the states.

33. 1960s.

34. There are more women working, fewer children per family, more single people, and more single heads of households.

35. By developing new products and flexible benefit plans.

36. People are both having fewer children and living longer.

37. Many employers are adding long-term care insurance and post-retirement medical insurance benefits to their group pension plans.

38. A social movement supporting the rights and powers of buyers in relation to sellers.

39. a. Insurers have developed coverages that address consumer needs.

    b. States have enacted laws mandating minimum health insurance benefits and confidentiality of medical care information.

    c. Congress has passed legislation requiring that employers make continuation of coverage available for terminated employees.

40. The aging of the population, advances in medical science, greater availability of health care, greater awareness of health matters, and catastrophic illnesses.

41. • Aggressively controlling company expenses and improving efficiency and productivity;

    • improving underwriting to reduce losses;

    • requiring insureds to pay greater amounts in deductibles and coinsurance; and

    • shifting to managed care.

42. Shifting to managed care.

43. Insureds have moved to managed care plans and the cost-control techniques of managed care have been introduced into traditional insurance.

44. The greater the proportion of health care costs paid by the insured, the lower premiums can be.

45. a. The movement of more workers into part-time, temporary, and service sector employment.

    b. The increasing cost of health care.

    c. Laws mandating that certain coverages include certain benefits.

    d. The erosion of Medicaid coverage for the poor.

46. The increasing cost of health care.

47. Increasing costs have led to higher premiums, which has made employers less able to provide group insurance and individuals less able to pay premiums for either group plans or individual policies.

48. They make coverages more expensive.

49. Improvements and alternatives for consumers, a focus on service, negotiated discounted contracts with hospitals and physicians, and increased mergers and acquisitions.

50. • They create larger companies.

• They enable companies to move quickly into new areas with high growth potential by merging with or acquiring companies that already have operations in those areas.

• They allow companies to focus on their most profitable areas of business by selling off peripheral areas to other companies who are seeking acquisitions.

51. Mutual companies.

52. • Traditional insurers have moved into the managed care market by merging with or acquiring managed care organizations.

• Managed care organizations have moved into product lines new to managed care by merging with or acquiring companies specializing in those areas.

• Strong managed care organizations have acquired smaller managed care organizations in an effort to increase their presence in a particular geographical area.

53. An insurer forms a relationship with another company in order to do something better or to do something it could not do alone, such as provide a service or product or reach a certain market.

54. • Outsourcing of certain functions to other insurers or specializing firms;

• alliances between North American insurers and start-up companies in other countries, particularly developing countries; and

• private labeling.

55. A better known company sponsors and puts its name on the product of a less well-known company.

56. Specialty products, such as long-term care and disability income insurance.

Answers to Practice Exam Questions

1. a

2. b

3. d

4. d

HIAA'S SELF-STUDY COURSES AND PROFESSIONAL DESIGNATIONS

For more than 40 years, the Health Insurance Association of America's Insurance Education Program has offered current, comprehensive, and economically-priced self-study courses for professionals seeking to advance their understanding of the health insurance industry. Since 1958, more than 300,000 people have enrolled in these courses. Most enrollees are employees of health insurance companies or managed care organizations, but consultants, third-party administrators, agents, brokers, and other health insurance professionals also study with us. In addition, an increasing number of noninsurance professionals, including health care providers, economists, consumer advocates, and government officials, are taking HIAA courses to gain a better understanding of the operations of our industry and to advance their careers in their own fields.

Courses include:

- The Fundamentals of Health Insurance (Parts A and B)

- Managed Care (Parts A, B, and C)

- Medical Expense Insurance

- Supplemental Health Insurance

- Disability Income Insurance

- Long-Term Care Insurance

- Health Insurance Fraud

The completion of HIAA courses leads to two widely respected professional designations: **Health Insurance Associate (HIA)** and **Managed Healthcare Professional (MHP).** The HIA designation has been in existence since 1990 and is currently held by more than 16,500 professionals. The MHP, offered for the first time in 1996, is held by more than 4,000 designees.

For more information visit our website (www.hiaa.org) or call 800-509-4422.